PARENTING BEHAVIOUR AND CHILDREN'S COGNITIVE DEVELOPMENT

Parenting Behaviour and Children's Cognitive Development

Sara Meadows
School of Education, University of Bristol, Bristol, UK

Psychology Press
An imprint of Erlbaum (UK) Taylor & Francis

Psychology Press
27 Church Road
Hove
East Sussex, BN3 2FA
UK

British Library Cataloguing in Publication Data

A catalogue record for this book is available from the British Library

   ISBN 0-86377-402-4 (Hbk)
   ISSN 0959-3977

Printed and bound by Biddles Ltd., Guildford, Surrey

Contents

CHAPTER ONE

Introduction

This book arises from my concerns as a psychologist working with teachers and parents who are concerned with improving the education which young children receive in their schools and in other social settings. My own commitment to this practical goal is accompanied by an older and perhaps more fundamental interest in how to understand cognitive development on the one hand and parenting on the other. In earlier publications (Meadows, 1983, 1986, 1993; Meadows & Cashdan, 1988), I reviewed the field of cognitive development in the years of childhood and found that although the questions surrounding the issue of how and to what extent children's interaction with other people affects their cognitive development were clearly important, they were not so clearly examined, let alone so clearly documented, as to provide us with a good understanding of what happens, why, and what a responsible society should seek to do about supporting and improving it. The purpose of this essay is first to consider the theoretical and metatheoretical issues in the field, and second to marshal and evaluate evidence which can contribute to a firmer understanding. I will do this by providing an account of the theoretical argument and empirical evidence for "social constructivism" in cognitive development, and testing this against two major counter-arguments. This critical approach does not indicate a lack of commitment to social constructivism; rather, it indicates a commitment to take it seriously, and thus to examine how it works and what its limits are.

The final section of my last book (Meadows, 1993) ended by making a number of points which I want to address analytically in this essay. It is necessary to begin with these, because in an area of such complexity as the association between parents' behaviour and children's cognitive development, it is important to spell out and test some very fundamental assumptions about, among other things, the nature of human nature, the nature of culture and the nature of the research effort. While some of these will seem to be truisms, the complexity of explaining cognitive development in the light of the important contributions made by adults is so great that it seems crucial to follow the good examples provided by Piaget and Vygotsky and try to set out one's paradigms first.

1. Children do their thinking in a world which presents a particular set of physical, social and conceptual problems in a particular range of settings and experiences. What makes for successful thinking depends to a large extent on the problem and its context. "Good" and "poor" performance are, to a considerable extent, situation-specific. Both the specificities and the general characteristics of "good" thinking need to be elucidated. There is a wide range of possible criteria for "good" thinking. Some are, in an obvious way, provided by culture; others appear more universal (for example, coherence, or flexibility, or compliance with the rules of logic), though on examination the "culture-free" nature of many of these is debatable. Further questions need to be asked about how these criteria are manifested in performance; perhaps one important characteristic of good cognitive development is an ability to use cognition both generally and differentially across tasks and contexts.

2. The point that there are different sorts of good and bad performance renders untenable the idea of "development" as uni-dimensional progress from less advanced to more advanced functioning, for example more "complex" cognition. Evolutionary theory makes the same point. In general, evolution has led to more complexity only if more complexity has led to a higher degree of reproductive success. Development may lead towards better success (though it by no means always does so), but what "success" is and how it is reached will depend on the environmental challenges an organism meets and on the resources it has to deal with them. Phylogenetically, it may be important to retain some flexibility or variation in the gene pool (or the cognitive repertory during ontogeny) to call on if the demands of the environment change.

3. As well as there being different sorts of good performance reached by different paths, different paths or different means may lead to the same end, more or less efficiently or effectively or happily. We need to beware of what I will call "cognitive chauvinism", the assumption that

our own way of doing something is normal and best. We should also perhaps avoid assuming that the formally perfect model is always a good representation of what is actually done; "competence", or the heuristic that would lead to a perfect solution, and "performance", or the less formally perfect behaviour which is actually employed, may be cousins rather than identical twins.

4. Given this co-variation of context, performance and development, what may be important for cognitive development is the availability of a range of alternative strategies and the ability to select between them as appropriate to the particular situation. People whose repertoire of strategies is very limited or inflexible may do very well if they only encounter familiar problems, but much less well if a problem demands a new or modified strategy. This implies that cognitive processes have to become somewhat independent from the contexts in which they were first developed, to become at least potentially autonomous and consciously accessible tools. This probably requires conscious and deliberate application, and a willingness to exert effort and take risks; thus metacognition and motivation may be enormously important. Moving from being scaffolded by a more expert person to being able to support one's own cognition is an example of increasing autonomy in cognition. The process will never be complete, and cognition is always embedded in a context.

5. If cognition is initially part of a "context" and becomes somewhat independent of it but is never completely so, it will be necessary to examine the context, to identify the features which are preserved and which differ in new contexts, to examine the possibility or impossibility of transfer, to clarify, indeed, what in the person–process–context nexus is best attributed to what. As I will discuss, there are some theorists who see development as independent of context, and others who see it as constituted by it. Researchers also differ in how they seek to assess "context".

6. It is a common belief, which may be true, that one of the main candidates for a strong decisive influence on the content and effectiveness of cognitive development, and its speed, is the context of social interaction provided by the child's interaction with significant adults, especially parents. Certainly, human evolution has involved neoteny, a clinging to immature forms and a requirement for learning rather than instinct, which has made parental investment in offsprings' development essential for successful survival. It has been argued (e.g. Humphrey, 1976, 1983) that human language and cognition evolved to serve social purposes, to make possible the long-term interactions, relationships, cooperation and competition of the social group and to store and transmit its complex representations of information. As well

as these fundamental skills, there is evidence that much of cognitive development in childhood involves the acquisition of culturally specific cognitive skills through social interactions such as apprenticeships, pupillage or observation. It may perhaps be possible to *describe* cognition without this social development, but it will have to be included in explanations, and in educational enterprises.

7. That part of cognition may be socially constituted opens up interesting possibilities. For example, socially based cognition may be more advanced than cognition which is more separate from the social world. Cognition which is done socially may be more effective than solitary cognition; inter-individual discussion, and intra-individual reflection with oneself as one's own partner, may be extremely valuable. Potential changes in society through changes in parenting and in education are another, reciprocal, set of possibilities.

8. The social world being emotional, there will also be intimate links between cognition and emotion in development. Self-concept and motivation, very much part of the consequences of social interaction, will affect and be affected by cognition. An exclusive focus on "cold" cognition and an assumption that people can turn on cognitive skills unaffected by their emotions, their motivations and their understanding of the social setting in which testing takes place, will be seriously misleading.

9. Furthermore, the possibility raised by sociologists (e.g. Mayall, 1994) has to be acknowledged: the social settings in which children's cognitive skills are developed may constrain and exploit them, as well as help to expand them. The skills and understandings, the behaviours and the representations of knowledge that adults encourage in children may be selected because they benefit adults rather than children; so may the ways in which they are offered. The organisation of schools, for example, with a teacher:child ratio of 1:30, requires the child to learn to be a self-educator in ways which would not be necessary if the teacher:pupil ratio was 1:1. Similarly, the information technology revolution has added new content to the curriculum, and the mastery of a new range of skills is required. This is a point with many ramifications, most of which will not receive further attention here.

10. Despite the importance of social facilitation of cognitive development, and of cultural tools for cognition and of cultural demands for cognition, the main "machine" with which we think is built and run as part of a genetically programmed body subject to the laws of biology. The training that a culture provides for its members works on a brain which expects environmental input of all sorts and integrates it with its own endogenous programmes. The brain is dependent on experience for its development, both the experience which all brains could "expect" to

receive for the fine-tuning of pre-programmed development, and less expected experience for the building-up of more idiosyncratic neural networks which differ more between individuals. The question of how inside and outside forces interact is complex, controversial, intractable and endlessly fascinating. I will sketch two accounts of this interaction in this essay, though I do not think they as yet answer the question.

These are not new points, but they are not perhaps as clearly considered in mainstream developmental psychology as they might be. Sometimes this is because in order to construct a researchable question (even more problematic to construct a fundable one), epistemological complexities have to be put to one side in favour of using a simpler paradigm. Sometimes, however, these simplifications introduce a bias which distorts understanding and can come to impoverish the field. I think that this has happened in the case of cognitive development; Piagetian theory, a child-centred approach with immense merits but the major demerit of marginalising other people's contributions to an individual's development, has flourished and been criticised, and other competing approaches have followed, with different strengths and weaknesses. In this confusion between paradigms, there is a danger that assumptions will be implicit rather than questioned, that paradigms will be adopted or rejected rather than carefully tested, and that data drawn from one approach will not be drawn on appropriately for other approaches. I believe that this has happened in the study of cognitive development, and that the issue of how adult–child interaction contributes to the development of cognition is one where a critical analysis and synthesis of paradigms is timely.

In order to address these issues, which are very much at the meeting point of several prominent theories of development and a range of difficult conceptual and methodological issues, I will provide an evaluation of certain crucial epistemological assumptions as embodied in the Piagetian, Vygotskian and information-processing paradigms; review psychological research documenting the patterns of association between adults' behaviour and children's cognitive development; and draw them together in an attempt to understand what would be required for an adequate account of cognitive development as a biological and cultural phenomenon. The next chapter reviews models of cognitive development which focus on what is going on inside children's minds as they develop new cognitive structures. It is followed by an account of neo-Vygotskian "social constructivist" theory, which focuses more on adult–child interaction as a major source of cognitive development. There is then a review of some of the relevant data on parent–child interaction, especially interaction which could be described as neo-Vygotskian "scaffolding". This is followed by an examination of recent work which emphasises the genetic roots of parents' impact on children; this reinforces the importance of precision in specifying how parents have an effect on children, and suggests alternative causal chains may also be influential. Chapter 6 uses data from parent–child interactions which do not fit the "mainstream" pattern of scaffolding to test whether its benefits are as clear as the neo-Vygotskian theorists suggest. The final chapter provides a recapitulation of important points, and an overview of how parent–child interaction is implicated in cognitive development.

CHAPTER TWO

Theoretical perspectives: Cognitive development as primarily endogenous

INTRODUCTION

It must be the most fundamental question regarding the psychology of cognitive development: What models are appropriate for cognition? Are we best thought of as "in essence limited capacity manipulators of symbols" (Siegler, 1983, p. 129), so that simulation by computer is a central research strategy, perhaps even more important than looking at real humans; or as biological organisms with a long evolutionary history which has led us to have a brain which functions in particular ways and leads to particular cognitive activities, just as we have evolved lungs to breathe in a particular way, livers with a particular range of digestive powers, and a thumb articulated with fingers so that fine grasping is possible; or as members of social groups taking part in relationships and in cultures, and using and developing our cognition within them and inseparable from them?

Different models of human nature make different decisions about the relative importance of these models, whether to prioritise the social, the biological or the formal, whether to think of cognition as computation or adaptation or acculturation. Each model has enabled us to inch towards improved understanding of cognition, but each has its costs as well as its benefits.

The big divide, I think, is between those models where development is largely asocial and predominantly endogenous, and those where it is socially constituted or exogenous. There is a basic philosophical divide here which places Hegel on one side and Kant on the other (see, e.g. Markova, 1982); or, in contemporary work, at one extreme we have nativist theories postulating innate ideas (e.g. Fischer & Bidell, 1991; Fodor, 1981, 1983; and see also Plomin, 1994b; Plomin & McClearn, 1993) and at the other we are essentially constituted by our society (e.g. Bronfennbrenner & Ceci, 1993; Mayall, 1994). Most developmental psychologists agree that "cognitive development" involves change from a starting point which includes some innate predispositions, if not ideas, towards later states which vary in their content and in their sources, and that this change comes about largely through an active engagement of the individual with the physical and social worlds; however, emphases within this general agreement differ considerably. The debate in the psychology of cognitive development is embodied in the work of Piaget and Vygotsky. Each acknowledged that cognitive development is both endogenous and influenced by the outside social world, and each admired the other's work even when there were disagreements, but they developed different emphases, particularly regarding the role of adult–child interaction in the development of the child's cognition (Glassman, 1994; Van der Veer & Valsiner, 1991). I will outline their theories in turn. Piagetian theory has been understood as marginalising the role of adults in children's cognitive development, and so might be judged to be irrelevant to this essay, but an understanding of this child-centred approach is essential for an appreciation of the strengths and the problems of theory which takes the alternative approach and centres on adults' contributions to children's cognition.

PIAGETIAN THEORY AND ADULT–CHILD INTERACTION IN THE DEVELOPMENT OF THE CHILD'S COGNITION

Piaget emphasised the biological nature of cognition, seeing it as one form of the general struggle for "adaptation" to the environment which is characteristic of all living organisms and at the heart of evolution, with the motive forces for this struggle being seen as predominantly endogenous. The Piagetian organism owes its development primarily to an innate and inevitable drive to adapt to its environment, through assimilating new information to the structures of knowledge which have already developed, and accommodating its existing structures of knowledge to accumulating new information. It is equipped with a need to "equilibrate"; that is, to maximise consistency, to eliminate contradiction and to ensure coherence in what it knows. It develops through equilibration's orchestration of three disparate things: physical maturation, primarily of the brain; reflection on its experience of the physical world and of the logical rules which can be applied to it; and finally and marginally, social interaction. The last factor is the least emphasised in Piagetian theory. The main form of social interaction which he saw as contributing to cognitive development was conflict with one's peers. This could lead to a recognition that one's own ideas were disagreed with by someone like oneself, and therefore might potentially be disagreed with by oneself too. (Equilibration is also, and more importantly perhaps, driven by the recognition that one actually disagrees with oneself, in an entirely endogenous cognitive conflict.) This recognition of a potential internal conflict is what prompts further reflection, and the revision of old ideas. Piaget (1932, 1968, 1983) implied that disagreement with someone unlike oneself would not have this effect of sparking off an internal disagreement, because it would not be recognised as potentially one's own problem. Disagreement with an adult, especially correction by an adult, would have little benefit for true cognitive development both because adults are viewed as different by children and because the power difference complicates things; the Piagetian child may bow to the adult's authority to the extent of parroting the correction, but will not internalise it. The result of adult instruction in the Piagetian model is limited; it gives rise to passive copying of what the adult has said is right, which does not become integrated with what the child has worked out independently, and may be even more damaging in that it may prevent the child from discovering for him or herself what the adult has taught.

> In some cases, what is transmitted by instruction is well assimilated by the child because it represents in fact an extension of some spontaneous constructions of his own. In such cases his development is accelerated. But in other cases, the gifts of instruction are presented too soon or too late, or in a manner that precludes assimilation because it does not fit with the child's spontaneous constructions. Then the child's development is impeded, or even deflected into barrenness, as so often happens in the teaching of the exact sciences (Piaget, 1962, p. 246).

(This particular example is interesting because Vygotsky, as we will see, made a case for the reverse in the development of scientific concepts, arguing that formal instruction enriched the child's independently developed informal scientific concepts and that science could and should be taught. Bryant (1995) makes a similar point about young children's arithmetic.)

The main thrust of Piaget's argument was, then, that children can only profit from social interaction if they already have the relevant cognitive structures, that social interaction can only complete their development, not create it. Conflict is more important than confirmation, and relationships which are unequal in competence and status cannot result in an improvement in cognitive development because the junior partner, the child, will not be able to be an active partner in resolving disagreement. Young children will be especially unable to profit from social interaction because they are too "egocentric" to recognise that there is a disagreement, and so will not notice that there is a cognitive conflict. Premature teaching is likely to distort and impede development. All in all, this is a picture of cognitive development that marginalises adult–child interaction; adults are at best marginally able to facilitate by providing materials for the child to explore, but may be dangerous intruders and distorters of development if they try to teach.

Piaget also insisted on cognitive development being uniform across individuals in the sense that they would all develop their cognitive structures in the same sequence despite differences in social milieu; such differences could lead to individual differences in rate of progress through the stages, and to minor differences in the detail of the content to which structures are applied, but not to major differences in the sequence or the overall structure of stages. Such developmental processes as accommodation and assimilation were "functional invariants", uniform across all cognitive development, indeed all adaptation between individuals and their environments. Cognitive development was seen as a sequence of unreserved improvements. The later developing forms of cognition, formal operations for example, were clearly "better" cognition, more differentiated, more complete, more inclusive and more flexible (Piaget, 1978, pp. 30–38). The theory asserts that everyone goes though the same sequence of development, and though there may possibly be some who do not progress so far towards the most mature forms of cognition, the main component of individual differences was a difference in the speed of progress from the sensorimotor stage to the formal operations stage. This was due mainly to the effectiveness of equilibration and the individual's opportunities for more or less reflective abstraction—essentially, a model of endogenous individual differences. Cognitive structures, moreover, fitted together tightly in the Piagetian model, so that uniformity of level of skill was to be expected except at times of transition from one stage to the next, when a degree of slippage or "decalage" could be tolerated for a brief period. This view of cognitive development as being universal in its content and variant only in its rate, and also as being a linear progression towards a single better form, is a profound rejection of culture as a component of cognition. It is also, I think, heavily dependent on a notion of evolution itself as convergent progress towards a "higher" form, a model which derives from the Social Darwinists' mis-understanding of Darwin's own work and which current views of evolution would reject.

This view of cognitive development pushes social interaction so far into the background that it has been barely visible in most popular versions of Piagetian theory. It has been the subject of much debate and challenge by subsequent researchers and commentators (see, e.g. Bovet, Parrat-Dayan, & Voneche, 1989; Doise & Mugny, 1984; Meadows, 1983; Perret-Clermont & Brossard, 1985). Certainly, it is not universally accepted that intra-individual conflict is better for cognitive development than inter-individual conflict, or that conflict is better than cooperation and confirmation, or that symmetrical relationships give rise to more progress than asymmetrical ones; there is probably a consensus that the learner should engage actively with the new task or information rather than passively memorising what is new, but even passive reception, an extremely non-Piagetian way of learning, has been seen to produce some development. Differences in research design may have caused some of the inconsistencies in the results of neo-Piagetian studies of the effects of social interaction. Younger and older children may differ in their openness to social facilitation of learning, as Piaget himself suggested, though not necessarily for the reason he suggested, as the degree to which young children are truly egocentric is also a matter of disagreement (Cox, 1980). The assessment of changes in cognition during training studies is also problematic: If the criterion for the effect of the intervention is advancement leading to the successful performance of a task, then smaller (or different) advances, such as a longer period of working on a task even though the right solution is not forthcoming, or understanding the solution when someone else provides it, may not be looked for, even though they may be more likely consequences of a short exposure to social interaction.

Debates about theories of cognitive development tend to neglect the possibility that the strengths and weaknesses of different theories may arise in part because they apply to different areas. Theorists of cognitive development differ, simply and obviously, in what content they are discussing. Piaget focused mainly on achievements such as conservation and class inclusion, using familiar materials that are universals, developed by most individuals whatever their culture, background or level of intelligence. He had nothing much to say about less general content, such as reading, formal science, or art history. Presumably, in so far as these cognitive activities use general processes, they could be seen as developing via equilibration and the rest of Piaget's fundamental processes; beyond this, their idiosyncracies would be acknowledged as culturally given but dismissed as largely uninteresting. Vygotsky's position, as we will see, allows both the universal and the culturally specific to be of interest. There may be symptoms here of the perennial debate about the position of psychology somewhere between biology and sociology, though I do not wish to address that argument here. However, if our cognitive contents differ as to whether they are universal or idiosyncratic, general or specific, it may be worth considering whether there are different acquisition processes for different components. Recently, biologists (e.g. Gottlieb, 1983, 1991; Greenough, 1991; Greenough & Black, 1992; Greenough, Black, & Wallace, 1987) have made the distinction between "experience-expectant" brain development, which uses universal experience to fine-tune a largely genetically programmed neuronal development with early critical periods, etc., and "experience-dependent" neuronal development, which uses—and is to a degree constituted by—less predictable stimulation that has not been general enough in our evolutionary history for development to be able to take it for granted. Piagetian developmental processes and structures may perhaps be more appropriate descriptions for the former than the latter: the Vygotskian developmental processes which will be discussed later may suit the latter more than the former.

The considerable body of work on neo-Piagetian accounts of social interaction and cognitive development does not tell us when and how social facilitation of Piagetian cognition occurs. Nor does it explain how socially induced learning is incorporated into endogenously powered developmental progress. Assimilation, accommodation and equilibration presumably do all the work here as elsewhere, perhaps with some built-in subordination of the exogenous to the endogenous. One has the feeling that the truly Piagetian child, even if told how to do it, would insist on re-inventing the wheel. Whether or not this is so, other people are seen as essentially the same as the non-social parts of the child's environment; they facilitate cognitive development if they induce cognitive conflict, and their own goals and intentions are no more important to the theory than the child's are. Cognitive development is free of emotion apart from the discomfort of being in a state of cognitive disequilibrium, and its main motivation is the internal tidy-mindedness of equilibration, adaptation and organisation. As I shall argue, there are important points about the functions of cognition, both presently and during the earlier stages of our evolutionary history, which make this set of assumptions problematic.

KARMILOFF-SMITH'S THEORY OF
COGNITIVE DEVELOPMENT

Piaget's marginalisation of adult–child interaction in cognitive development makes his theory less helpful than it might otherwise have been to the enterprise of examining the nature and effects of such interaction. The same is true of most information-processing accounts of cognitive development (for reviews, see Meadows, 1993; Siegler, 1983; Sternberg, 1984). Here the emphasis is so much on what is going on within the individual, and the model is so clearly the computer, which normally has only the most impoverished of social contexts and of adult–child interaction, that it is hard to apply much of this work to children's discussions with their significant adults. An interesting recent account of cognitive development (Karmiloff-Smith, 1992, 1994), however, does give some hope for a *rapprochement*.

Karmiloff-Smith (1991, 1992, 1994) presents a model of cognitive development that seeks to combine Piagetian and connectivist features. She criticises nativism, arguing that a Piagetian epigenetic interaction allows true development that begins from rather more initially existing innate predispositions and constraints than Piaget supposed. She replaces the Piagetian account of general coherent stages of development with a "phase" model, in which similar changes occur during the development of different domains but without the requirement of synchronicity across domains that the Piagetian model required. She argues for domain-general processes of learning through the successive redescription of domain-specific representations. Her emphasis is on representational redescription as an endogenous process, though she does acknowledge the possibility of exogenous influences.

While in some senses Piagetian, it is clearly an information-processing account, as the focus on representations and their redescription clearly indicate:

> Development and learning, then, seem to take two complementary directions. On the one hand, they involve the gradual process of proceduralization (that is, rendering behaviour more automatic and less accessible). On the other hand, they involve a process of "explicitation" and increasing accessibility (that is, representing explicitly information that is implicit in the procedural representations sustaining the structure of behaviour) (Karmiloff-Smith, 1992, p. 17).

The representational redescription (RR) model attempts to account for the way in which children's representations become progressively more manipulable and flexible, for the emergence of conscious access to knowledge, and for children's theory building (Karmiloff-Smith, 1992, p. 17).

Karmiloff-Smith describes a series of ways of representing information. The first is *implicit*, essentially procedural or enactive; the child is able to solve a problem or perform a task correctly only if there is no attempt to analyse it or to vary the procedure. It is impossible, for example, to begin midway, or to recover from failure except by starting again from the very beginning. The child learns to represent the information which the external environment supplies, adding new representations of information to the existing stock without amending it. The representations remain specific to the particular task or domain and are comparatively piecemeal. They eventually give rise to consistently successful performance, generated by the sequence of independently represented components of the task's solution: first this is done, then that, then that, and so on. The children who nudged blocks into balance in her balance task (Karmiloff-Smith & Inhelder, 1974–75) had this sort of implicit representation.

In the next phase of learning, there is a move towards representations which are to some degree *explicit* and accessible to deliberate reflection and modification. The implicit representations of the first phase are subject to internally generated change, where the child's own system of representations dominates the knowledge modification process. The new level of representations may lose perceptual detail, but their reduced descriptive detail is made up for by more cognitively flexible conceptual information; for example, the implicit representation of the individual queen, president or daddy is subsumed under a generic representation of the qualities and attributes of heads of state or parents. The implicit representations continue to be available for use with cognitive goals requiring a swift, automatic response only, such as recognising who is coming towards you and whether to bow, salute or embrace them; the redescribed representations are necessary for goals requiring explicit knowledge, such as discussion of etiquette, respect and affection. Redescription may be done while the task is being solved "on-line", or outside the task context, rather than while the task is being done; it is caused by internal pressure to assimilate and accommodate rather than by external task demands.

The first explicit re-representations, E1, involve explicitly defined representations which can be related to other representations and otherwise manipulated, but are not necessarily verbal or accessible to consciousness for report. They go beyond the procedurally embedded implicit representations of the first phase and can be marked and manipulated and contradicted (for example, in pretend play), but until they are re-represented once more into accessible representations (E2) or verbally describable ones (E3), they remain somewhat inchoate. In moving from one phase of representation to the next, the learner recodes information which is stored in one code or form into a different code or form; for example, the movement-based map which enables one to navigate successfully along a familiar route may be re-encoded into a visual sequence and then into a directionally coded one. Each redescription is a more condensed version of the information that was stored in a more concrete form before. The earlier levels remain to some degree, and may still be used for appropriate purposes; they may also be influenced by changes in the later representations. An example from my own experience might be helpful. I remember the disorienting effect of the redecoration of the Psychology Department where I was an undergraduate. Two years as a student had sufficed to build up a proprioceptive procedure for getting from one point to another, and a visual sequence and a verbally accessible direction-specifying one. However, the change in the visual representation that followed the redecoration threw the proprioceptive representation, and I felt in danger of colliding with walls, and recoiled from empty spaces, markedly enough to remember it years later. The verbally accessible "straight on, then right, straight on, first door" description remained intact, but never felt like a guide to my own movements.

Karmiloff-Smith suggests that whenever a new domain or task is addressed, there will be a sequence of mental descriptions and redescriptions of what must be done to solve the task, or of what the domain is. The initial representations will be implicit; once a level of behavioural mastery is reached and success is consistent, re-representation at successively more explicit levels will ensue. The process of re-representation is general across domains, extracting information contained in the stable mastered understanding of a particular domain so that it can be used more flexibly in other areas. Questions of analogy presumably arise here. The degree to which representations have become explicit will vary however from domain to domain, depending on how far there has been progress towards mastery. Karmiloff-Smith (1992, p. 26) also claims that "it is from the repeated process of representational redescription, rather than simply from interaction with the external environment, that cognitive flexibility and consciousness ultimately emerge".

Clearly, Karmiloff-Smith is saying here that cognitive development is dependent on endogenous processes, centrally among them a consensus-based version of equilibration. Exogenous processes are freely acknowledged but not otherwise dealt with, and the ideas of

Vygotsky and Bakhtin about "dialogicality" and "multivoicedness" (see next chapter) are not considered. However, there would appear to be no reason of principle why the internal processes of representation and of representational redescription should not incorporate other people's representations, and how, when and why this is done is one area in which the theory could be developed.

Both here and elsewhere, Karmiloff-Smith makes a strong case for taking "development" seriously. She points out that if the goal is to understand human cognition, it is necessary to examine its built-in architecture and constraints on learning, and how knowledge changes over time. A developmental perspective makes these concerns especially prominent, and thus has much to offer cognitive science; provided it does not become "non-developmental", either by postulating that everything is innate and does not change over time, or by becoming bogged down in age differences without explaining why things change as age changes. Conversely, Karmiloff-Smith points out the merits of computer-based models for studies of development; generally because they provide a precise description of the phenomena under study, and focally because of their spotlight on the initial architecture of cognition, the processing mechanisms applied to information, and the way in which the internal representation changes. Given her preference for endogenous change, the impoverished social and cultural context of most computers is not a problem. The lack of a biological context, perhaps even more important, remains a problem (see, e.g. Bates & Elman, 1993; Edelman, 1994).

The representational redescription model is neutral with respect to whether there are innate specifications of, or domain-specific constraints to, development. Her examination of how children come to be mature linguists, physicists, mathematicians, psychologists and notators (users of writing and drawing) suggests that there are innate predispositions, and that development can proceed more or less independently in different domains. She retains Piaget's epigenetic or constructivist view of cognitive development, while differing from him on his assertion that it is general across domains and independent of innate specifications. There would seem to be very general processes, such as representational redescription, which are applied to many domains, but there are no domain-general stages of change, as representational redescriptions proceed according to mastery of the particular domain concerned, and may be at very different levels in domains where the child's expertise varies. There may be a very successful procedural mastery of how to produce a winning serve in tennis and an inability to state it verbally, coupled with a well-articulated representation of what to do with one's income from this profession; equally well there could be a fluent armchair analysis of why a serve had failed, coupled with a procedural inability to begin to produce it oneself. Here, in these discrepancies, influences from other people's representations may be particularly marked; the fine-tuning of many skills will be strongly influenced by our mentors' views. Possibly, too, the sequence from implicit representations to increasingly explicit re-representations might in some senses be reversed, if the inital representation that was adopted was the adult's verbal one, and automatic enactive representation followed later.

The nativists argue that children develop in very similar ways (for example, they believe that similarities in the timing and even sequence of content of language development are very marked, though Bates et al., 1995, show that there are problems with this position) because they have in common the same basic prespecified mental structures (or modules). The environment is minimally required as a trigger. But this view drawn from similarities neglects two points. First, there are real similarities in the environments that children inhabit, which might themselves contribute to the apparent uniformity of development; second, there are certainly subtle differences in development which deserve more attention than they have been given by those nativists who have dismissed them as measurement error. The purpose of this essay is to begin an examination of these subtle variations in development and to make the case that their effects are not always so subtle as to be unimportant for development, but that they are often major determinants of children's development and their life chances.

Karmiloff-Smith concludes her 1992 book with an interesting statement—that the human mind is unique in its ability to build complex representations, which it represents explicitly and so makes them usable beyond the special-purpose goals that they were originally used for. This manipulability of representations enriches the cognitive system, and adds exploitation of one's own whole body of knowledge to the exploitation of the information immediately presented by the environment. Representations of information from a domain are built up to solve the problems which that domain presents; but as the domain task is mastered, representations within the domain and between it and other domains are compared, contrasted, coordinated, synthesised and subsumed into a flexible and creative system. Increasingly they become accessible to metacognitive attention; increasingly, too, I would add, they become accessible to the activities of teaching and learning from being taught. There could be a role for other people's representations in the development of one's own; this, too, would be something which is unique to humans, or at least particularly well developed in the human mind.

Karmiloff-Smith adds an interesting account of external notations to her account of internal representations. Even within the mind–brain system there are probably both alternative representational formats and multiple representations of the same information, for example the different mappings of visual information in the visual cortex. These may be focused on different aspects of the information stored, or may be accessed differently for different sorts of use or report; they are not necessarily mutually linked. Similarly, a variety of notational formats is available, culturally given in the outside world. These can enable the mind–brain system to transcend its limitations by extending its representations and making them potentially more available to others. Like internal representations, different notational systems have strengths, weaknesses and costs that make them more or less suitable for particular tasks.

Children meet many notational systems in the culture that surrounds them; in fact, most cultures have devised notations for most of the things they wish to have represented. Among these familiar cultural tools are writing, maps, mathematical notation and musical notation. Karmiloff-Smith acknowledges that external notation systems are appropriated as part of the child's cognitive development, and that as well as enhancing cognition they change the structure of the brain and the nature of the internal re-representations that the individual has formed. She describes a study by Peterson, Fow, Snyder, and Raichle (1990), which measured event-related potentials (ERPs) in the brains of adults, 4-year-olds and 7-year-olds who were asked to scan written letter strings to detect a partially thickened letter. All the subjects showed an amplification of right hemisphere activity in response to the task, but only the adults showed a right–left asymmetry. The children were not yet fully literate, while the adults were, so these results suggest that the brains of literate and not yet literate people respond differently during a literacy task. The appropriation of the external notation system of written language may lead to a reorganisation of parts of the brain. As improvements in the measurement of brain activity increase our understanding of how the brain works, more evidence of this kind of change may emerge.

Although the emphasis of the model is clearly on the endogenous representation of mastered problems or domains, Karmiloff-Smith does acknowledge that the child is surrounded by other people's representations, and that these may be explicitly offered to the child as "better" representations and the basis for re-representation. Other people's models can be a source of representation for oneself, perhaps through inital imitation leading to enactive implicit representation, which is then transformed in increasingly explicit re-representations just as a representation that had always been endogenous might be; or perhaps through a reverse sequence of some sort where the parroted adult representation of the knowledge is somehow incorporated into a successful enactment. (Vygotsky's discussion of scientific concepts, which I mention later, could be an example of this bidirectional development.) This remains an unanswered question, and a particularly interesting one for psychologists concerned with parent–child interaction and with education. In the next chapter, I use Vygotskian ideas to examine this.

Karmiloff-Smith's discussion of re-representation is perhaps foreshadowed by Hegel's account of knowledge being acquired through a "circle returning within itself" (Markova, 1982), a process which clearly consisted of successive redescriptions of the object being known, which successively modified the individual's state of knowledge. The initial phase of coming to know something is vague and implicit, often enactive; in the process of knowledge acquisition, more information is incorporated, but not additively, in that each change involves reappraisal of all that was there before. The eventual representation is more explicit, more concrete but also more flexible. The process of knowledge development is creative, reflexive in that it continually works itself over, and is always in the context of the task and previous experience. Thus, it is inextricably part of the historical, social and cultural context, which both prescribes and prohibits certain tasks and provides possible ways of solving them. Thus the communication of knowledge to oneself and other people becomes important.

I have argued that neo-Piagetian and information-processing models are limited in their contribution to our understanding of cognitive development in so far as they exclude the social components of development. Karmiloff-Smith's work shows that such approaches are not necessarily incompatible with social constructivist theories. The next chapter describes neo-Vygotskian theories of cognitive development, which offer an alternative account of how other people's understanding becomes one's own, and begins to test these theories in turn against the principles of development that I set out at the beginning of the book.

CHAPTER THREE

Theoretical perspectives: Cognitive development as largely exogenous

INTRODUCTION

Piagetian theory, and the information-processing theories of cognitive development for which Karmiloff-Smith's interesting account stands as an example, focus primarily on sources of cognitive development which are asocial, and thus have little to say about adult–child interaction. The third major account of cognitive development, however, that of Vygotsky, places adult–child interaction of a particular sort right at its focus. It is thus to neo-Vygotskian theory that I turn next.

Piagetian theory insists that there are psychological structures in people's minds which are invariant across cultures, settings and tasks, and essentially independent of the individual's relations to other individuals, to social practices, and to the cultural environment: and thus that psychology is the study of the idealised individual mind's inner workings, which are seen as developing through individual maturation or learning, or individual construction of an internal model of outside reality. Vygotsky provides a radical challenge to this model. Far from being internal and individualistic, cognitive abilities are formed and built up in large part by social phenomena: they are public and intersubjective, created largely through interaction with the social environment. Any description or explanation of cognition and cognitive development which isolates them from the social interaction that constitutes them is seriously incomplete and may provide a distorted and misleading picture.

This is true, incidentally, of all of the development of the individual. Throughout ontogenesis, multiple forces of development are in operation simultaneously.

> The cultural development of the child is characterised first by the fact that it transpires under conditions of dynamic organic changes. Cultural development is superimposed on the processes of growth, maturation, and the organic development of the child. It forms a single whole with these processes. It is only through abstraction that we can separate one set of processes from others. The normal growth of the child into civilisation usually involves fusion with the processes of organic maturation. Both planes of development—the natural and the cultural—coincide and mingle with each other. The two lines of change interpenetrate one another and essentially form a single line of sociobiological formation of the child's personality. (Vygotsky, 1960, p. 47, cited in Wertsch, 1991, p. 22).

SOCIAL INTERACTION AND COGNITIVE DEVELOPMENT: VYGOTSKY'S MODEL

For Vygotsky, the higher forms of cognition originate in social interaction and centre on children's appropriation of cultural tools, goals and activities, which they internalise in coming to be full members of the culture. Interaction with other people, especially more skilled people who take the responsibility for facilitating the child's learning of cognitive skills, and who use language and non-verbal teaching strategies to do this, is crucial. The more expert partner takes responsibility for the task initially, structuring it so that the child is able to participate in increasingly complex ways, letting the child undertake more and more of the task autonomously, and eventually handing over responsibility to the child when all the actions necessary for the task can be performed and put together successfully. Ultimately, this "scaffolding" is internalised so well by the learners that they can provide it for themselves in new tasks. The learning child learns not only how to do the particular task, but how to learn; that is, he or she learns how to observe, analyse, imitate, monitor, scaffold, review one's own activities, or indeed other people's, as the erstwhile learner becomes able to teach the skill to new novices. The neo-Vygotskian model of teaching centres on scaffolding; the model of learning involves the repeated use of a wide range of processes, from mindless imitation to reflective abstraction of general principles of metacognition.

Vygotsky's assertion is that cognitive development involves the internalisation, transformation and use of cognitive routines, concepts and skills which surround the child in the activities of fellow-members of the culture (and also embodied in objects, for example books, computers, maps, clocks). These routines, concepts and skills are learned socially, through observation and imitation of the work of more skilled and competent partners. A child is enabled to develop sophisticated cognitive repertoires despite only having rudimentary skills him or herself, because adults who developed the sophisticated routines and concepts earlier are able to guide the child repeatedly through the appropriate behaviour. The child does not have the resources necessary to function at a high level, but adults do. An adult and child interact, the adult providing the structured context within which the child can act as though competent to solve the problem, and by thus acting in this supportive and restricting context the child is enabled to do the right things and so reach the solution successfully. To begin with, the adult provides almost all the cognition required for the task, but as the child comes to be more and more familiar with it, the adult can leave more and more for the child to do, until at last the child can undertake the entire task successfully. Repetition of this scaffolding is necessary for learning each complex task, and repetition on related tasks extends the child's competence and eventually leads to an ability to take on new examples with minimal—or even no—adult support. The child has learned to provide a self-scaffolding. The child's independent cognitive behaviour has become more sophisticated and expert, and the medium of development has been social interaction, apprenticeship to another, more skilled, person.

Cognitive development is to be understood in terms of the child being implicitly and explicitly trained to behave in ways which the culture has developed as cognitively useful. By so behaving, and by practising and reflecting on what is being done, the child internalises the cognitive skills of the culture and can develop them and pass them on to the next generation. The child is helped by the adult in the appropriation of the accumulation of knowledge and ways of thinking that preceding generations have constructed. The skills required of the child include observation and imitation, and generalisation and decontextualisation, but even these fundamental skills develop under the fostering support of social interaction. Some of the skills learned are what Bruner (e.g. 1990) called "cultural amplifiers", cognitive tools which make certain thinking jobs easier. Other cultural habits of thinking may impede cognitive development in general, though they are highly serviceable within a confined cultural domain. Whether helpful or not, the culture's cognitive tools surround children, are modelled to them by other users and in some cases discussed with them, and they may structure their language, their play, their schooling and their social interaction. The developing thinker does not have to create thought out of an unpeopled vacuum, but will adopt and eventually internalise some of the cognitive content and processes provided by others. It may be hard to avoid doing so, as so many cultural amplifiers have become all-pervasive; different ways of representing experience, for example the passage of time (Kozulin, 1990), change historically and structure our experience day-to-day.

BIOLOGICAL DEVELOPMENT AND COGNITIVE DEVELOPMENT: VYGOTSKY'S MODEL

This is not to deny two important points. First, the cognition of infant, child and adult has roots in our existence as biological (and indeed physical) systems. The quotation from Vygotsky given above shows his recognition of this (see also Van der Veer & Valsiner, 1991). This interplay of biological and cultural works in two ways. Ontogenetically—that is, in the development of the individual—there may be very early behaviours that arise in any intact human whatever the culture he or she grows up in, which are in an important sense precursors of later cognitive achievements. Babies' ability to recognise that two consonant sounds are different is found very early (Aslin, Pisoni, & Jusczyk, 1983) and forms a basis for the later discriminations of a true language user who knows the difference between "bad" and "pad". But the social world quickly modifies such abilities: Children who grow up in a language community whose language does not use the physical difference between two phonemes which as babies they could register, for example the difference between the "t" in "top" and the "t" in "stop" which is not noticed in English, come to lose the discrimination which was present earlier. In an even more clearly mediated social effect, pointing is initially an unsuccessful reach towards a desired and too-distant object, which is responded to by the baby's caretaker as a sign that the baby wants the object. The baby's movements are interpreted as a gesture indicating what is desired. As the caretaker comes to the baby's aid and delivers the reached-for object, the movement of reaching that was initially a gesture "in-itself" becomes a gesture "for-others". The caretaker, by treating it as such, has made it a social gesture. The child, associating the unsuccessful reach with caretaker behaviour that delivers what was wanted and was not obtained by the reach directly, comes to use it to induce the caretaker behaviour: the reaching becomes reduced to movements that could no longer achieve the desired object even if it were within reach, but signal economically to the caretaker that the object is wanted and the baby wants the caretaker to hand it over. Thus where the younger baby looked and reached, and then found the object delivered by the caretaker, the older baby looks at object and at caretaker, cries, whines, points, says "please will you get it for me because I can't reach", and so forth. The child addresses a modified form of the biologically given action to the adult who may bring about the desired result, rather than directing the reach to the non-social object, which was the first focus of interest. The distinction made between "experience-expectant" and "experience-dependent" brain development is helpful here; some brain development is merely fine-tuned by the small variation in detail that exists in the normal environment and can be "expected" to occur at the right time in the developmental process, but other development is left more open to experience, to be determined to a significant degree by experiences which vary a great deal between individuals so that no single version can be confidently "expected" to occur. Adult–child interaction is more likely to be an important determinant in the latter case than the former.

The second way in which the biological nature of the species has to be considered is in the way in which our physical nature defines our cognition. Despite the millennia of heated debate about the relationship between "mind" and the brain, there are few certainties; but one of these is that cognition is dependent on the functioning of the brain and nervous system, and so the anatomy, functioning and development of the brain have to be taken into account in attempts to describe and explain cognitive development. A description of cognition which ignores brains, or would require them to do things which all the neuroscience evidence in its increasing richness suggests they could not do, is based on shaky foundations. It may be one of the advantages of the "connectionist" models that are currently being developed (see Bechtel & Abrahamsen, 1991; Clark, 1989; Minsky, 1988) that they have a better fit to our rapidly developing knowledge of the brain's development and functioning than earlier artificial intelligence (AI) did. Neuro-physiological studies document continued physical changes in brain circuitry as a result of learning throughout life; connectionism suggests a continual building-up and reconstitution of knowledge and skills as a result of new input which modifies the existing representations in the cognitive system.

It has been argued (e.g. Bronfenbrenner & Ceci, 1993; Humphrey, 1983) that another aspect of our biological nature, or, more precisely, our evolutionary history, has significantly affected our cognition. Human beings have to attend to a variety of stimuli and respond in a variety of ways. Unlike some other creatures, we have not evolved into specialists who can rely on instincts to carry them through the limited number of situations they need to address, nor into the sort of creature that reproduces itself in such quantity that only a small proportion of the offspring need to survive to adulthood to carry the genes into the next generation. Rather, humans have fitted themselves into a great variety of ecological niches which provide adaptational challenges too varied and too demanding for pre-programmed instincts to supply solutions. They have also developed a reproductive strategy which produces minimal numbers of offspring per litter, and offspring which are far too immature at birth to be able to fend for themselves. Getting these offspring to adulthood requires a heavy investment in parenting if they are to survive at all; they also need to learn the many ways of surviving that their unpredictable environments demand. An important part of this is learning to cope with the demands of the social environment, which for many individuals may be the most complex and challenging part of their ecosystem. The existence of a social world which predates the child's individual experience may offer a short cut to competence because he or she can profit from other people's experience—you don't have to be bitten by a dog to know that dogs may be dangerous—but it also adds on requirements, for example that you should know what your culture regards as acceptable behaviour *vis-à-vis* dogs; are they edible, for example, can they be allowed to roam freely and defecate at will, can you use them to hunt other animals and, if so, which. In order to make these sorts of adjustments, evolution has provided us with a large and complex brain that retains a capacity for learning right through our lives; and with a context for our development as individuals that surrounds us with other people who are already versed in the ways of the culture and have an interest in acculturating us. Models of cognitive development should contain an adequate recognition of this if they are to provide adequate explanations of development.

Besides the need to recognise the strengths and limitations that our physical and biological nature gives us and our cognitive systems, it is also important to recognise that disembodied, asocial models of cognition may make important contributions to our understanding of it. Information-processing theorists who use computer simulation, for example, find its pressure for precision and specificity aids them in producing a clearly operating artificial intelligence. While we are still uncertain of how real human brains work, this model-building may be an essential tool; and even with much more knowledge about brains, it will be useful to operate on more than one level of description. There is no point in hoping for a reductionist account of cognition in purely neural terms, and formal and social descriptions will be needed to complement the biological ones. What is needed is attention to the ways in which different levels of description can interface with each other, including a recognition that the different levels serve different functions and differ in their field of relevance.

PROCESSES OF COGNITIVE DEVELOPMENT: VYGOTSKY'S MODEL

Vygotsky's account of cognitive development as a result of social interaction solves the "bootstrapping problem" of explaining how more sophisticated cognitive competences could arise from less sophisticated ones. It is hard to see how a child might solve everyday cognitive problems, such as realising that a word picks out a particular aspect of an object, without previously having a whole complex of concepts about that object. A word can become a name, or a label, for an object, only against a background of beliefs about what might be being picked out by the word; how can a naive listener know that a word such as "cat" refers to the type of object rather than its colour, noise or position? One solution has been to say that cognitive processes and concepts are innate, or at least the result of innate biases to carve up the world in particular ways (Fodor, 1981; Gelman, 1990); another has been to find "precursors" of the full-blown behaviour in the hope that these will form a sequence of credibly small steps. Vygotsky's solution, radically, makes innate ideas unnecessary and small steps part of a social learning process. Children can develop more sophisticated cognitive competences despite only having simpler ones in their own repertoire, because the adults available as teachers or models have the more sophisticated competence in their repertoire to guide the children through the relevant behaviour. The child as an individual does not have the skills and resources necessary for the task, but the combination of child and adult does. Tharp and Gallimore (1988, p. 14) provide a familiar but telling example:

> A six-year-old child has lost a toy and asks her father for help. The father asks where she last saw the toy; the child says "I can't remember." He asks a series of questions—did you have it in your room? Outside? Next door? To each question, the child answers "No." When he says "in the car?", she says "I think so" and goes to retrieve the toy.

At the heart of this development is the process of "internalisation". Vygotsky gives a more detailed and precise exposition of what internalisation is than many other psychologists have done. It is primarily seen in the context of the social interactions of the learner.

> All higher mental functions are internalised social relationships ... Their composition, genetic structure, and means of action—in a word their whole nature—is social. Even when we turn to mental processes, their nature remains quasi-social. In their own private sphere, human beings retain the functions of social interaction (Vygotsky 1981, p. 164).

This may mean that the child comes literally to enact the role of the other, providing the questions, prompts, supports and feedback which earlier came from the adult tutor. Wertsch (1991) presents data from a 2½-year-old child and her mother who are working on selecting pieces from a pile to fit together to make a replica of a model. At an early stage, the sequence involves the mother taking a lot of responsibility for leading the child with helpful questions, instructions and comments:

1. Child (C): Oh. (C glances at the model puzzle, C looks at the pieces pile.) Oh, now where's this one go? (C picks up a black piece from the pieces pile, C looks at the copy puzzle, C looks at the pieces pile.)
2. Mother (M): Where does it go on this other one? (C puts the black piece she is holding back down in the pieces pile. C looks at the pieces pile.)
3. M: Look at the other truck and then you can tell. (C looks at the model puzzle, C glances at the pieces pile, C looks at the model puzzle, C glances at the pieces pile.)
4. C: Well ... (C looks at the copy puzzle, C looks at the model puzzle.)
5. C: I look at it.
6. C: Um, this other puzzle has a black one over there. (C points to the black piece in the model puzzle.)

The child seems to know that she should look at the model and copy puzzles, and at the pile of pieces, but her glances are seen by Wertsch as cursory, and purposive only after her mother's question and instruction (utterances 2 and 3). She still does not see where her mother's utterances are directing her. In a second episode, the sequence still shows shared responsibility, but with more competence on the child's part:

7. (C glances at the pieces pile, C looks at the copy puzzle, C picks up the orange piece from the pieces pile.) Now where do you think the orange one goes?
8. M: Where does it go on the other truck? (C looks at the model puzzle.)
9. C: Right there. (C points to the orange piece in the model puzzle.) The orange one goes right there.

The child's initial question about where a piece goes is still followed by a helpful response from the mother which leads, again, to the child consulting the model. In a third episode, the child provides this response for herself, and the mother has only to confirm the child's own solution of the problem:

10. C: (C looks at the pieces pile, C picks up the yellow piece from the pieces pile, C looks at the copy puzzle.) Now how ... Now where ... Now ... (C looks at the model puzzle.)
11. C: You ... You ... the yellow on that side goes ... One yellow one's right next there. (C points to the yellow piece in the model puzzle, C looks at the yellow piece she is holding in her hand.)
12. M: Okay.

In this third episode, there seems to be "inner speech" by the child which provides what the mother had previously had to do for her. Wertsch (1991, p. 88) glosses this in the terminology developed by Bakhtin: there is "hidden dialogicality", "the statements of the second speaker [here the mother] are omitted", but the "second speaker is present invisibly"; her "words are not there, but deep traces left by these words have a determining influence on all the present and visible words of the first speaker [here the child]". The child's responses to the "unspoken words of another person" are now abbreviated inner speech; earlier the child solved the problem in a dialogue with her mother, now she does so in a more fragmented dialogue where she plays the internalised dialogic partner as well as her original role of learner looking for guidance. Or, more subtly, her "turns" may "presuppose" the other turns of the partner who is now internalised. Rather than performing both parts—her own overtly, her internalised partner's subvocally—the partner's turns are much abbreviated and not fully represented in her mind, although they do influence strongly how her turns run.

(Wertsch's discussion here focuses primarily on verbal behaviour and the child's direction of her gaze towards the puzzles. No record is presented of the mother's non-verbal behaviour. This reflects the field's normal focus on verbal mediation of cognition. The work of Rogoff and her colleagues (see below) suggests that this is potentially a significant omission, in that the non-verbal contribution made by the mother in this sort of setting may be an important contribution to the child's success. Certainly, the child's shift from "glance" to "look" here suggests that there are changes in the sophistication of her non-verbal behaviour as well as in what she says.)

This is the process which Bakhtin calls "dialogization" (Wertsch, 1991). As cognitive processes move from being interpersonal to becoming intrapersonal, cognition becomes increasingly dialogical, or multivoiced. The adult cognitive person may be acting in a solitary setting, in a room by herself with her word-processor, but what is written (or uttered) is multivoiced as process and as content. It is composed in a sort of dialogue between herself as author and herself as the anticipated reader, and also between herself (as reflecting on other people's texts and utterances) and those people (as represented by their utterances and texts), and it is full of other people's utterances and ideas, sometimes unmodified, sometimes abbreviated, occasionally transformed. Despite our cultural emphasis on individuality and on creativity, few if any texts are free from this sort of dialogue.

Dialogicality also implies that neither spoken nor written communication is a one-way transmission of information from utterer to receiver. Understanding is a dialogue, where "for each word of the utterance that we are in the process of understanding, we, as it were, lay down a set of our answering words" (Wertsch, 1991, p. 73, quoting Voloshinov). Two voices come into contact and interanimate each other. Senders are influenced by past and future receivers; receivers by past and future senders. The message can and does function in more than one way; it both conveys the communication's meaning (perfectly only when the roles and understandings of the speaker and the listener coincide completely) and it gives rise to new meanings. In the latter case, it is "multivoiced" or "dialogic". Thus it can generate new understanding and new texts.

The argument of Vygotsky, Bakhtin and Wertsch, then, is that cognition and dialogue are normally "multivoiced", and that this is necessary for communication between people and for the "individual" thinker, who is not so autonomous as has been supposed. Cognitive development is centrally the appropriation of the ways of thinking that other people foster in the child. Children participate in the cognitive problems and use the cognitive tools which their culture makes available to them. They gradually internalise the cognitive process into an inner dialogue. "Internalisation" may involve taking on the role of the more expert partner in a very literal way. Brown, Bransford, Ferrara and Campione (1983, p. 124) summarise the nature of an expert learner thus:

> mature thinkers are those who provide conflict trials for themselves, practise through experiments, question their own basic assumptions, provide counter examples to their own rules, and so on. Although a great deal of thinking and learning may remain a social activity, mature reasoners become capable of providing the supportive-other role for themselves through the process of internalisation. Under these systems of tutelage, the child learns not only how to get a particular task done independently, but also learns how to set about learning new problems. In other words, the child learns how to learn.

"Internalisation" and "dialogicality" might appear to involve a form of identification. The child acts as much like the more skilled other as possible. This should not necessarily be taken as a wish or an effort to impersonate or become the other; rather, the learner is copying the actions of the expert because the expert's actions have been seen to achieve a result which the child also wishes to achieve. If the child can discover or invent other means to achieve what the expert achieved, these new means may be used instead; or even, if the expert is still around, taught to the original tutor.

This point about the tension between individually developed concepts and concepts learned as a result of formal educational activities is illustrated by work on scientific concepts—and also in children's early arithmetic, as Bryant (1995) shows. Children typically develop many concepts about scientific principles from their own experience before they are formally taught any science; notions of what will float, for example, are derived from innumerable experiences of objects and fluids long before there is any formal explanation of density. Vygotsky (1986) compared the spontaneously developed and formally taught concepts that children had. The taught ones were more formal, logical and decontextualised, more coherent and rigorous, but they lacked the rich base of experience and the connection with other concepts that the spontaneous concepts had. The two types of concept interacted in development:

> In working its slow way upwards, an everyday concept clears the path for a scientific concept in its downward development. It creates a series of structures necessary for the evolution of a concept's more primitive, elementary

aspects, which give it body and vitality. Scientific concepts, in turn, supply structures for the upward development of the child's spontaneous concepts towards consciousness and deliberate use (Vygotsky, 1986, p. 194).

This looks like a description of re-representation of concepts, perhaps comparable with the account of re-representation offered by Karmiloff-Smith (1991, 1992, 1994). It would seem, then, that Vygotsky, Piaget and the information–processing tradition agree on the importance of such a process. Disagreement remains, however, about the sources of re-representation and hence about whether it can be facilitated by social interaction.

Representation of cognitive activities is an important part of another Vygotskian concept. The "zone of proximal development", or ZPD, is defined in the course of a discussion of the interaction between "learning" and "development":

The zone of proximal development ... is the distance between the actual developmental level as determined by independent problem-solving and the level of potential development as determined by problem-solving under adult guidance or in collaboration with more capable peers (Vygotsky, 1978, p. 86).

Independent problem-solving indicates what cognitive functioning the child has already mastered; problems which the child can only solve with assistance suggest what functions are still immature but are in the process of becoming ready for independent use. There is little point in offering scaffolding below the bottom of the ZPD, because the child can already function here without it, or above the top of the ZPD, because the difference from the child's present functioning may be too great. Within the ZPD, adult–child interaction is likely to facilitate development, though it may do so in a sequence of different ways. During the earliest periods of learning in the ZPD, a child may have a very limited understanding of what the task involves; the teacher offers a model or successive precise and simple directions, and the child merely observes or imitates. Gradually, as the child is able to cope with more components of an activity, and has a greater understanding of how they fit together—an understanding that includes more appreciation of what the goal is and how best to reach it—the adult reduces the assistance given and changes from very directive help to suggestion and encouragement. The adult needs to take less and less responsibility for the successful performance of the activity as the increasingly competent learner takes it on. As they become competent on the task, the bounds of the ZPD move onwards; the erstwhile learners scaffold their own performance of the task which is now below their ZPD, and the teacher scaffolds the next level of tasks. Eventually, even self-regulation becomes so well learned that it is no longer observable, except when extraordinary task difficulty or the need to teach learned skills to a new novice make it necessary to employ conscious control and description again. Tharp and Gallimore (1988) and Tudge (1990) describe the implications of the ZPD for the reform of classroom practice.

The idea of the ZPD as the area where interaction with more skilled others is most likely to change cognition is an interesting and important one. It would be an exaggeration to say that it has been thoroughly tested empirically, so it would be premature to conclude that it is easier to learn or better to teach entirely within the ZPD. Even diagnosing it precisely is not altogether straightforward, as a skill which does not seem to be within a child's grasp given one sort of help, might be if the child is given another. However, Vygotsky's discussion of it resonates in interesting ways with other notions in cognitive development—with Karmiloff-Smith's discussion of redescription of mental representations, for example. And such characteristics of individuals' ZPDs as their width might be important components of individual differences; a very narrow ZPD, with the child showing very little profit from adult help, might lead to either slower or more Piagetian learning than a wider one, where the child learns a great deal with adult support.

SUMMARY

I think that cognition (both mature cognition and the course of cognitive development) emerges from these theoretical models as a complex portfolio of different processes, acquired through a range of different developmental changes which co-occur in as yet unspecified ways. It may be helpful to attempt a listing. There are clearly processes which are very close to properties of brains; for example, some memory processes, associative processes such as are found in connectionist models, ways of perceiving speech sounds, etc. These seem to be almost universal, provided the brain is undamaged and receives the "normal expectable" amount of relevant stimulation at the right time. They are not, however, necessarily equal between individuals; for example, although current conceptualisations of "brain speed" (e.g. Anderson, 1992; Eysenck, 1993) are very crude, they may be a real source of individual differences in intelligence and cognitive development. Expectable experience fine-tunes these universals; it also makes at least some of them available for re-representation, meta-cognition, teaching/learning, etc. Much of cognition, and most of the "higher processes", uses these basic processes but in more deliberate, conscious, meta-cognitive, socially constituted ways. Some of this may be universal (e.g. conservation), whereas some may not (e.g. doing long division). Development will always involve processes such as Piaget described, because brain maturation, experience of the physical world, experience of other people and some sort of endogenous tidying-up (which we may call equilibration, or use information-processing terms such as consistency detection, contradiction resolution or representational redescription) go on all the time and cannot but impinge on the development of cognition. But much cognition is part of the social fabric which is also being woven (and unpicked and repaired) all the time; and the more that cognition facilitates social life, or is among the goals of a society's acculturation of its members, the more it will be constituted by social interaction. If a society has developed over the preceding generations a valued way of doing a cognitive task or of representing reality, it will seek to induce such behaviour or representations in its child members. Here the brain development involved may have depended to a considerably greater extent on "experience-dependent" growth. The detail of what is known, of how things are understood, of what associative weights there are on items in a connectionist network, of what can be done easily or with effort or not at all, will vary and will have involved both endogenous processes and social ones such as imitation and interaction. Descriptions of both endogenous and exogenous processes of learning and development are needed, as is analysis of how they come together in development.

This general outline of how cognitive development must be built up now needs some fleshing out. My intention is to move towards this fuller account and the possible contribution made by adult–child interaction. So far, most of what has been said derives heavily from theoretical considerations, and perhaps from a definition of psychology as "the science of mental life". In the next chapters, I want to move towards data and to psychology as "the science of behaviour".

CHAPTER FOUR

Parent–child interaction as a source of cognitive development: Empirical studies

INTRODUCTION

We have seen that considerations drawn from both evolutionary theory and the psychological theory deriving from Vygotsky's work place adult–child interaction in the position of a prime mover of cognitive development. My concern in the rest of this book is to examine this theoretical claim by marshalling evidence for and against its importance. But there is a complexity that must be acknowledged at this point. Interaction between adults and children is part of their wider experience of living in a particular culture at a particular historical moment and in a particular physical environment. What is done, and what is supposed to be done, will differ according to these as well as according to the other specific characteristics rooted in the participants. Cognition and language are areas of potential development which cultures have strong interests in controlling. Most of those reading this book, like most of those researching in this area, will be used to late-twentieth century, Anglo-American, middle-class value systems, their expectations of development, their ways of teaching children, their choice of what cognitive skills to require, to encourage and to proscribe. When discussing the formative influences of adult–child interaction in cognitive development, it is essential to recognise that there are cultural differences in both input and outcome. These are both interesting in themselves and a useful window on the causes of development.

This chapter presents studies of American and British samples first, looking at what has been discovered about associations between parent–child interaction and the child's development of cognition, including language, numeracy and literacy. There is then a brief review of some cross-cultural material, and the chapter ends with a summary of the case to that point.

SCAFFOLDING

Setting aside for the moment the very important points that cultures differ in how they support children's cognition and that we should not succumb to the cultural chauvinism which only recognises our own way of doing something, what do we know about the effects of scaffolding, which is clearly the culturally valued version that our chauvinism would advocate? A number of studies have looked for effects directly, and I will discuss these here; others, using slightly different research strategies, are discussed later.

Various researchers have made detailed observations of adults (usually mothers) working with their children (usually preschoolers) on a task such as drawing a pattern (Hess & Shipman, 1965), assembling a puzzle (McNaughton & Leyland, 1990), constructing an object to match a model object (Wertsch, 1979, 1991; Wertsch, McNamee, McLane, & Budwid, 1980; Wood & Middleton, 1975; Wood, Wood, & Middleton, 1978), reading a book (Pellegrini, Perlmutter, Galda, & Brody, 1990), number tasks (Bryant, 1995; Saxe, Guberman, & Gearhart, 1987), or other various sorts of games and problems (Freund, 1990; Heckhausen, 1987; Hodapp, Goldfield, & Boyatzis, 1984; Kontos, 1983). Both the content and the sequence of contingencies between the participants were examined. In most but not all of these studies, the child's later independent performance was better if the adult had provided some approximation to "scaffolding" than if the interaction had been more one-sided. As "scaffolding" is potentially such a complex package of behaviours, it is important to look carefully at what sort of behaviour was involved.

Scaffolding and problem-solving
In David Wood's studies (Wood & Middleton, 1975; Wood et al., 1978), 4-year-olds and their mothers were observed as they assembled a wooden pyramid. The mothers were asked to teach the children how to put the pyramid together and the children were finally assessed on their independent performance. The complexity of the construction was such that a child of four could not complete it alone, but could succeed if given

appropriate support. Mothers varied in how well they provided supportive instruction, and their style of teaching affected how well the children learned to do the task; that is, how complete the pyramid was when at last the child was asked to do it alone. The mothers who taught most effectively, in that their children performed best when left to do the task alone, seemed to use two "rules" to guide their behaviour. If the child failed to succeed with a given level of help, then the level of help or control was increased and a little less left to the child's responsibility. If the child succeeded at a given level, then the next instruction might offer a little less help, and give a little more responsibility to the child. Failure was followed by reducing the risk of failure slightly, success by slightly increasing task demands. Similar sequences appear in the data of other researchers, for example the studies of Wertsch (1979, 1991; Wertsch et al., 1980) quoted earlier, and in studies of children being taught to read (e.g. Pellegrini et al., 1990; see below) and to begin arithmetic (Bryant, 1995; Saxe et al., 1987).

Studies like Wood's show that mother–child pairs differ in the quality of scaffolding, and that pairs where there is child-contingent sequencing of demands seem to give rise to especially effective learning. Saxe and co-workers' (1987) account of number games suggest that negotiated problem-solving is a fairly common experience for both middle-class and working-class American children. Here, mothers matched the type of instruction they gave to how difficult the child was finding each subgoal of a task, giving more specific instructions on harder tasks and more complex instructions to older and more accurate children, and making instructions more specific after the child made an error. Many children succeeded on the task when working with the mother, being able to adjust their behaviour in correspondence with their mother's instructions; they could thus achieve more complex goals in interaction than they could alone. Children were interested in arithmetic from an early age. Their ability to generate numerical goals enabled their participation in social activities using number, and mothers scaffolded this participation so that the children achieved more in partnership than alone. They thus came to understand goals more advanced than their own, and this facilitated understanding enabled participation in still more complex goals and interactions.

The children in the studies of Saxe and his colleagues were interested in mathematical work and were being scaffolded by their parents into various mathematical activities. Part of this social facilitation involved them learning the cultural tools of elementary arithmetic, including the number name system. Bryant (1995) has recently argued that in children's early arithmetic, a good self-generated understanding of operations such as sharing, adding and subtracting, developed to a considerable degree before schooling begins, has to be grafted on to the number system which is culturally provided. Cultures differ in their number name systems, and some systems facilitate exact representation of numbers and exact numerical calculation more than others (see, e.g. McLeish, 1991). It seems that children whose culture provides them with a really regular and ordered system of number names are better at a range of arithmetical tasks, from the simple one of producing numbers in sequence to more complex addition sums and simple problem-solving. Learning the decade structure of numbers is essential for much complex calculation, and for understanding various useful mathematical tools such as decimals. Children have to combine this learning, which is an important part of the school curriculum, with the understanding that they develop more informally in other contexts.

One of the problems which mathematics educators face is that children can pick up quite different forms of mathematical skills and understanding in different contexts, and have difficulty transferring understanding from one context to another. A very interesting body of work on Brazilian children who worked as street vendors illustrates this (Carraher, Carraher, & Schliemann, 1985; Nunes, 1992; Nunes, Schliemann, & Carraher, 1993; Saxe, 1988). These children could work out the prices their customers must pay and the amount of change they must give in a rapid and error-free way, using algorithms of multiplication, addition and subtraction flexibly and easily. On equivalent problems in a more formal setting, their calculations were more rigid and much less successful. This sort of dislocation between skill in one setting and skill in another, or between two different methods of doing the same calculation even in the same classroom setting, is common.

The social facilitation of children's number skills eases them into the culturally given mathematical systems that are made available to them (Lave, 1988; Stevenson, Lee, & Stigler, 1986). It is clearly an important route of access to mathematical understanding, but this is not to deny the existence and the importance of self-generated understanding (and constraints) such as Piaget described and researchers like Gelman (1990; Gelman & Gallistel, 1978; Gelman & Meck, 1983) have investigated more recently, and of a variety of components of mathematical understanding (Bryant, 1995).

Wood's experimental studies, and Saxe and co-workers' account of number activities, looked directly for associations between scaffolding as a moment-by-moment matching of the adult's behaviour to that of the child's and the child's learning, and found evidence of a child–adult–child sequence which could scaffold the child's achievement successfully. These are therefore interesting and important examples of scaffolding existing and facilitating children's development. Most of the other research evidence supports these findings, but generally with evidence that is further removed from the moment-by-moment sequence which occurred. Most studies tabulate how many occurrences of particular sorts of behaviour were found without looking so closely at which led to which, and therefore doubts about what caused what are more serious. These questions of cause are important and difficult, and I will return to them later.

Adult–child interaction and language development

Perhaps the largest body of popular belief and of psychological research on parent–child interaction and child development assumes that the main factor is the effect of the parent on the child. "Spare the rod and spoil the child", "build yourself a brighter child", "punish the parent for their child's delinquency"—all these assume a unidirectional effect of parent behaviour on child outcome. This was the dominant model for research on parent–child interaction for many years, perhaps because the unidirectional parent-to-child assumption simplified what was obviously going to be a complex problem into something more manageable. In the context of parent–child interaction and the child's cognitive development, most of the existing research focuses on language and far less on other aspects of cognition. Many studies (see, e.g. Bates, Dale, & Thal, 1995; Bornstein & Bruner, 1989; Ely & Gleason, 1995; Forman, Minick, & Stone, 1993; Garton, 1992; Harris, 1992; Ochs & Schieffelin, 1995; Snow, 1995; Stafford & Bayer, 1993) have traced associations between parent language as an input and child language as an output. Frequently, an association has been found between more maternal input and the more rapid development of the child's language, and various semantic and pragmatic features of the child's language have been associated with the mother's use of language, which is sensitive to both the child's present competence as a speaker, converser and cogniser, and to his or her engagement in both conversation and activity (e.g. Bates et al., 1995; Farrar, 1990; Hampson & Nelson, 1993; Harris, Jones, Brookes, & Grant, 1986; Hoff-Ginsberg, 1990; Murray, Johnson, & Peters, 1990; Snow, 1995; Tomasello, Conti-Ramsden, & Ewert, 1990; Wells, 1985). For example, Martyn Barrett and Margaret Harris and their colleagues have looked at the associations between mother's speech and the child's lexical development (Barrett, Harris, & Chasin, 1991; Harris, Barrett, Jones, & Brookes, 1988). They found that there was a strong relationship between maternal speech and the child's initial use of words, but that the subsequent use of these words was less correlated with the mother's use. This seemed comparable with Karmiloff-Smith's   suggestion   that   children   initially   adopt representations provided to them by the outside world, but that as these become internalised they form an autonomous basis for the child's later development, thus reducing the correlation between initial input and later behaviour. Researchers looking for associations between input and output may need to think carefully about the time pattern of correlations that they find. Very early in such a sequence of adoption and internalisation there may be large correlations as the child imitates the mother, but later as the child develops a representation of his or her own rather than reproducing the one learned from the outside world without varying it at all, the correlation between adult and child will probably decrease. Only longitudinal evidence from the whole sequence of learning will show what the roots (and routes) of the child's behaviour were.

A further complexity is that there may be stronger associations for some children than others. We do have to take seriously the possibility that there are different routes into language (and cognition) for different individuals, with different patterns of causation along the way (see Bates et al., 1988, 1995). A recent study by Hampson and Nelson (1993) illustrated this. They videotaped children's interactions with their mothers at 1:1 and 1:8, looking at which children developed language faster and slower over this period. There were differences in the mothers' language to slower and faster developers even at the earlier age, probably because the mothers were differentiating by the child's language ability even then. The children differed on the "referential–expressive" dimension that seems to emerge from studies of early individual differences in language (and seems to involve a contrast between language which involves analysis and discussion of objects, actions and language itself, and language which involves a lot of social formulae and unanalysed phrases, though it is not completely understood; see Bates et al., 1995). The more referential children enjoyed more social contact with adults and less with their peers, their mothers were less intrusive and the children developed faster. The mothers' language at 1:1 was significantly correlated with the child's language at 1:8 for the referential children and for the fast developers but not for the expressive children and the slower developers; more maternal references to objects and more object nouns, and more maternal repetition of the child's nouns, seemed to lead to a longer mean length of utterance (MLU) for the more rapid developers and the more referential talkers but not for the slower and more expressive ones. Hampson and Nelson suggest that perhaps non-expressive children make more use of their mother's language as a basis for their own development, and that the mother's naming of objects is effective for enabling the child to break into the language system earlier. If the child is focused on learning names and information about objects in the environment, then a mother who produces more labels and more descriptions, repeats the child's labels and uses fewer empty conversational fillers, is likely to be a helpful model. A child whose bent is towards expressive language and is using language which fits the social and interpersonal context may make more use of such features of maternal speech as its prosodic patterns, but as no such variable was examined in this study we cannot say whether the expressive children were more advanced in these areas. Of course, both expressive and referential uses of language have to be developed, and almost all individuals function adequately in both; but referential language use seems to be especially highly correlated with cognitive functioning, perhaps because it is more useful for the expression of the results of cognition, particularly in formal testing and education, or perhaps because it can become a specially effective cognitive tool for the analytic, abstracting, disembedded and individual thinking that is valued in our culture.

Children's syntactic development has been said to be less closely linked to input language (e.g. Furrow, Nelson, & Benedict, 1979; Pinker, 1994), though some associations have been found (e.g. Farrar, 1990; Goldin-Meadow & Mylander, 1990; Hoff-Ginsberg, 1990; Snow, 1995). However, the explanation of this association is not a matter of consensus. Controversy still rages, even in the comparatively well-documented areas, mainly in the form of disagreement between those who see parent behaviour as a minimally important trigger to the innate development, which is the really important thing, and those who see parent behaviour as the constituting, motivating and determining cause of development. First, it is clear that children who receive no language from other people do not develop language themselves, though they may do so when rescued and immersed in a language-using community (Skuse, 1984); second, children develop the language they hear used by other people who interact with them, and not other languages even if they hear them (Snow, 1995); third, in all languages there is a concern that children should learn to talk properly, and accompanying this there are special ways of talking to children, though these differ from culture to culture (McCabe, 1989; Ochs & Schieffelin, 1986, 1995; Pine, 1994; Richards, 1994; Sokov & Snow, 1994). Researchers differ on whether these special ways of talking to children are teaching language, or, more informally, merely facilitating it, or, even more residually, merely setting up interactions which give children good opportunities to practise the skills they would develop anyhow because of their innate programming. All these views can be found in the current literature.

The range of debate over the role of other people's input into children's language acquisition is reminiscent in many ways of the debate over cognitive development. There are theories which emphasise the role of the child's innate propensities and workings-out and de-emphasise the influence of other persons (Chomsky, Piaget, the information-processing modellers and hybrids of these); here language and cognitive skills are seen as universal, both across individuals and cultures and, to a considerable extent, across tasks and settings. Other theories emphasise the role of others in constituting children's development (such theories may generally be linked to the work of Vygotsky and Bruner). These typically go further towards the compromise position (which must be the correct one) that what was initially a matter of the child using both endogenous and already acquired skills to pick up external skills and internalise them to some degree, may become a melange of skills: some innate and genetically programmed, some developed independently of other people through one's own reflection, some adopted from the outside world and transformed by the process of internalisation, some adopted and never modified. I think we should avoid any attempt to divide these conceptually by calling the more endogenous ones "development" and the more exogenous ones "learning". No useful consequences follow from the distinction, even if it is tenable. In all this, the most interesting questions are about how the skills reach competence. Language development provides some examples.

The language that adults use with children—motherese, babytalk or, more preferably, child-directed speech (CDS)—differs in its features from setting to setting (see, e.g. Ochs & Schieffelin, 1995), which complicates the already difficult task of discovering which of its features are associated with differences in the development of child language. It appears that Western children who receive a large amount of verbal stimulation from their caretakers and which is related to the children's own activities and utterances, and is warm and responsive rather than overly controlling, tend to show comparatively rapid language development, with syntax perhaps being less facilitated than the semantics and pragmatics of language. Social interaction probably facilitates language as communication rather than language as a formal system; the underlying variables seem to be responsiveness, joint engagement and perhaps frequency. Adults who know the child well may "fine-tune" their language to the child's competence, acting as a slightly more advanced model, facilitating the child's imitation, ensuring maximum understanding and engagement. If they do, the child clearly influences what the adult does, and it would resemble Vygotskian scaffolding. It is not, however, necessarily the result of a deliberate effort by the parents to teach language:

for most of the time the relatively finely tuned modelling of meanings and forms that the frequency data reveal occurs incidentally, as adults carry on conversation with their children for quite other purposes—to control the child's behaviour in the interests of his safety and their joint well-being, to share in and extend his interests, to maintain and enrich their interpersonal relationship and so on. Success in achieving these aims requires that the majority of the adults' contributions be pitched at a level of complexity that is not too far beyond the child's linguistic ability. However, this is achieved quite spontaneously by most adults under the control of feedback from the child's comprehension and production and does not require deliberate attention. The tuning that occurs is thus as much a response to, as a determinant of, the sequence in the child's learning (Wells, 1985, pp. 380–381).

Snow (1995; see also Sokov & Snow, 1994) has reviewed issues in the study of child-directed speech. She points out that CDS from someone who knows the child well as a daily conversational partner typically shows fine-tuning to the child's responsiveness or attentiveness, and adjustments of a wide range of features, including prosody, phonetics, length of utterance and grammatical highlighting. Interlocutors who know the child less well, or have different interests from the familiar partner, show less finely tuned CDS; fathers and older siblings, for example, are less responsive to the child's immature utterances and suffer more breakdowns of communication (Barton, 1994). This characteristic of being harder to communicate with may of course be a necessary part of the child's experience—just as in the rest of cognitive development, children have to come to bear the major responsibility for their own language. Children who are developmentally delayed, for example children with poor vision or hearing and children with Down's syndrome or language disabilities, tend to be less active and effective in their spontaneous communication, and also to receive CDS that is more directive and less contingent on their own behaviour (Bishop & Mogford, 1993; Conti-Ramsden, 1994; Cromer, 1991). Thus they may have an environment which is less conducive to making good progress in their language development. Snow briefly describes an unpublished intervention study by Nelson and colleagues in which children whose language development was normal and older children with specific language disabilities (matched, therefore, for present language competence) were trained on grammatical structures using syntactic recasts. The older, language-impaired, children were the more effective learners, which suggests that the impoverished nature of the CDS they normally encountered itself impeded their development. (There appear to be parallels with the classroom experience of poor readers, here; see, e.g. Meadows, 1993.)

Vocabulary acquisition is perhaps one of the crucial components of building up the knowledge base on which cognition will depend. Snow's (1995) review makes it clear that very young children learn their vocabularies largely from CDS; both the frequency with which the word is heard and its place in an episode of joint attention to an object (for nouns), or of commentary on the child's ongoing activity (for verbs), seem to be important. Later in childhood, word acquisition is not so closely related to sessions where the adult is pointing out the object or the action being attended to, but there are still good examples of correlations between the child's later use of words and the mother's earlier input. For example, mother's use of mental state verbs to refer to someone's mental activities or to encourage the child to reflect was a predictor of the child's use of the same verbs a year later, at age three (Furrow et al.,1979; Furrow, Moore, Davidge, & Chiasson, 1992), and mother–child discussions of people's emotions, needs and wishes has been seen to be correlated with more sophisticated understanding and use of other people's emotions a couple of years later (Dunn, 1988; Light, 1979; Peterson & Siegal, 1995).

A number of points that are relevant to a consideration of adult–child interaction and children's cognitive development emerge from Snow's review. First, the conditions for and the content of learning can be very specific, as in the case of the somewhat different input that facilitates early noun acquisition and early verb acquisition, or the apparent effectiveness of conversation about people's mental states for the development of a theory of mind. Second, slower developers seem to receive less responsive and contingent interaction with more expert users, and to be further impaired by this, as in the case of deaf and blind children and children with Down's syndrome; the experience of children who are poor readers in the primary school is another example of this. Third, it appears more and more likely that frequency of exposure to an opportunity to learn may be very important, and a better indicator of likely progress than the proportion of such events; the use of reading books is an example of this. Fourth, the contingent, responsive character of Western CDS seems to be one of its most important features; but, as I discuss elsewhere, there are cultural variations in what CDS is like, and we need to guard against cultural chauvinism.

The centrality of "responsiveness" raises questions about the assumption of a uni-directional effect of the parent on the child. If the parent is responding to the child's behaviour, then the child is one of the determinants of what the parent does. Parents may well differ in their responsiveness to children, but children also differ in their ability to provoke useful responses. Studies of children's effects on parents, and of reciprocal effects, are needed. So are studies of children's communication with other partners; it appears, for example, that the emotionally charged conversations of young siblings can be potent sources of cognitive development (see, e.g. Dunn, 1988). Studies of groups where either the child's or the adult's responsiveness is impaired in some way may also be interesting. Finally, if we do find patterns of individual differences in children's behaviour that are associated with differences in adults' contemporaneous or earlier behaviour in our observations of what they do naturally, we cannot know how they were caused, or which caused which. Similarities may be caused by the moment-by-moment interaction, or by underlying similarities in genes, or by underlying similarities in cultural expectations: experimental studies, longitudinal research with carefully carried out measures of the timing of associations, and "experiments of nature" with groups who differ in known ways from the normal range will all make their contributions. Some discussion of such groups will follow later, after a brief discussion of adult–child interaction in the development of children's use of written language.

Learning to be literate

I have just argued that using spoken language is the result of a developmental process in which interaction with skilled language users is an important, indeed critical, component. In North America and Britain, experiencing a copious quantity of fine-tuned and child-contingent input from adults seems to be a major formative influence on children's language, a potent source of subtle but influential individual differences. Becoming literate may be even more clearly a product of being taught to use written language. What part does child-contingent responsive scaffolding play in this?

I must begin by acknowledging the effects of other influences. There are genetic influences on reading ability (Stevenson & Baker, 1987; see also the studies of Plomin and his colleagues discussed in Chapter 5), though these are less marked than for general intelligence. As well as this variation within the normal range of reading ability, which is no doubt associated with differences in intelligence, there is some reason to believe that some reading difficulties may be linked to a minor genetic anomaly. Thus genetic influences affect reading ability, both through their effect on the general intelligence which influences reading as it does all other cognitive activity, and their effect on certain specialised processes necessary for reading. An early history of delayed language development is a predictor of later difficulties in learning to read (Silva, Hughes, Williams, & Faed, 1987; Stevenson, 1984). A large number of reading difficulties are associated with problems of phonological processing (Bryant & Bradley, 1985; Goswami & Bryant, 1990; Hulme, 1987). Reading achievement is influenced by the opportunities for learning that are a product of family circumstances (Yule & Rutter, 1985), thus it is correlated with socio-economic status (SES) and birth order, and with poverty, overcrowding and housing conditions.

Besides these general indices of the child's experience, there are associations between experience of literacy and later literacy achievement. In some cases, these associations seem to be the result of differences in reading skills rather than their cause; children whose reading is progressing well are more likely to be given rewarding books to read and more likely to choose reading as an activity. A number of children teach themselves to read through a self-generated immersion in books (Clark, 1976), though in most cases there has been parental sponsorship of this activity even if the parents do not set out to teach the child to read.

It is clear that children who have difficulties with reading during the school years both miss out on the benefits that fluent reading has for amusement and information, and may suffer ill-effects on their self-esteem and reputation because they are failing compared with other children. Poor readers are likely to have problems with most school subjects (few school subjects make no demands at all on your ability to read) and to be regarded by their teachers as more anti-social, clumsy, inattentive and anxious than good readers (Rodgers, 1983). Reading failure is something better avoided. (It is, of course, easier to avoid it once you have moved out of the school setting; a lot of new coping strategies become available and consequently the long-term outcomes of developmental reading problems do not necessarily include anything like the degree of failure and stigma that was suffered in school (Maughan, 1995).) There has also been, however, a strong and wide-spread popular belief that parental reading to pre-school children makes a major contributor to their later reading development. It is clear that the interaction which surrounds reading storybooks could contain many opportunities for the young child to acquire knowledge about reading and books, to pick up positive attitudes to reading, and even to practise some of the skills of literacy. Children with less experience of being read to at home tend to exhibit somewhat poorer knowledge of literacy as they begin school and to make slower progress in learning to read (e.g. Wells, 1985). Recently, Scarborough and Dobrich (1994a, b) reviewed a large number of research studies and found that there is a moderate and fairly consistent association between reading to pre-school children and the development of skills of literacy and of language. Although the general literacy of the child's household also predicted development, and differences in shared reading may be part of the differences due to SES and to subcultural differences (e.g. Heath, 1983, 1986, 1989), the frequency and perhaps the quality of parent–child interaction with a book correlated moderately with the child's short- term and longer-term learning to be literate. Reading to children did seem to have a small but quite significant effect on their own later reading progress beyond what would be predicted from background variables, such as parents' intelligence and the general literacy of the household.

Scarborough and Dobrich found that the child's interest in literacy was also a good predictor of later literacy achievement. Hence it is possible that differences in shared reading and in progress in learning to read were merely a result of differences in child interest, which was the main causal variable in literacy achievement. This position would mean that children's characteristics caused both the quantity and quality of reading they were exposed to and their progress in learning to read. More probably, there would be a reciprocal relationship between interest and exposure, with children becoming more interested in books as a result of being read to, and also initiating more reading sessions as a result of their growing interest. The effects typical of intervention studies, where children's progress in learning to read has been improved by inducing parents to read more to their children, to read more responsively, and to support their child's own reading during the school years of learning to read by methods such as "paired reading" (Tizard, Hewison, & Schofield, 1982), support this position. Indeed, as the commentaries on Scarborough and Dobrich's paper argue (Dunning, Mason, & Stewart, 1994; Lonigan, 1994), it is unlikely that the parent could give the child story-reading experiences which facilitate reading without engaging the child's interest, or that the child could be interested in reading books without having been read to. However, the discussion in these papers reminds us again of the dangers of assuming a parent-to-child effect which is independent of other possible causal sequences. There probably is a small effect of parent input in the form of frequent stimulation by reading books to the pre-school child on child output in the form of the child's progress in learning to read, since such an association is found both in observations of ordinary parents and children and in a number of intervention studies where a change in parents' behaviour was followed by a change in the children's behaviour; but there is also input from the child in the form of interest and responsiveness. Other dimensions of behaviour, such as intelligence and spoken language abilities, and access to books at home and later at school, will also complicate the picture.

OBSERVATIONS OF ADULT–CHILD INTERACTION: CROSS-CULTURAL DATA

We have seen that there is a moderate amount of work from samples drawn mainly from the middle class of Western cultures that provides quite strong documentation of an association between parent–child interaction and the child's cognitive development. The causal sequence may be child–adult as well as adult–child, but there is prima facie support here for the neo-Vygotskian model of scaffolding as a facilitator of cognitive and linguistic development. In the next chapter, I will play Devil's Advocate, and see if alternative explanations for the association seem as strong. But before that, I must return to the point about cultural chauvinism I made at the beginning of this chapter, and offer a brief examination of the possibility that other cultures have different ways of facilitating their children's cognitive development.

One of the better documented fields is language development, and excellent recent reviews can be found in Lieven (1994) and Ochs and Schieffelin (1995). They argue convincingly that it is impossible to understand language development, even grammatical development, without serious analysis of the social and cultural milieu of the child acquiring language. (This must be even more the case in areas where there is less possibility of an innate specification for development.) Ochs and Schieffelin (1995) conclude that language development is an outcome of children's regular participation in socially and culturally organised activities, where participants value the language (or languages) and encourage children to become appropriate language users. They suggest that linguistic accommodations such as are characteristic of child-directed speech may be an outcome of the culture's view of childhood. Mainstream Western society sees even young children as having an important role as addressee and speaker, and provides novice language users with a great deal of support features, such as child- contingent speech, fine-tuning of syntax, pragmatic shifts towards prompting, repetition, display questions, and so on. In other communities, where children have the more peripheral role of overhearers and observers, there is much less adjustment of adults' behaviour to allow children to participate, and instead the children witness the normal complex activities of the community, being expected to learn about them through observation. Frequent exposure to ways of using language or cognitive skills is assumed to be sufficient for the child to become, eventually, competent; less special teaching, and less special provision of opportunities to learn, are thought to be necessary, compared with the Western tradition. The fascinating ethnographic work of Heath (1983, 1986, 1989) illustrates these differences in different groups in the south-east United States.

Lieven (1994) describes the evidence on the range of language settings in which children learn to talk, with their varying adjustments of adults' language to children's perceived needs, and addresses the difficult question of how these adjustments might relate to children's acquisition of grammatical structure. She points out that the range of language structure and use which children encounter is enormous, and generalisations are therefore dubious. Some children grow up in societies where they are merely eavesdroppers on adult talk, where it may be regarded as foolish or even dangerous for adults to talk to young children because of their immaturity or vulnerability. Western children who only hear speech which is not addressed to them or adjusted to them, and might therefore be seen as having the same low degree of exposure to CDS, seem not to learn language from their "eavesdropping". Children from cultures where adults do not talk to young children, on the other hand, do seem to learn language, presumably by using their eavesdropping. The crucial difference may be in the contrast between the Western child's more rarefied social contacts and the more continuous social interaction which surrounds all the members of the traditonal cultures which have been studied. Lieven suggests that children can learn to use language even if they have not often been addressed, if they are continually present in the social group, sitting on their mother's lap, watching and listening to their older siblings as they talk, observing the teasing, storytelling and word-play of the neighbours conversing on the doorstep. Children certainly attend to talk, and may be picking up information about how it works. They may begin to speak by imitating the ends of routine phrases, playing with variations on them, expanding them into multiword imitations, and being gradually received as participants in the group's language. Their close company with the social group differentiates them from Western middle-class children exposed to television in a foreign language or other utterances which have no social meaning.

Whereas Western children living in a dyad with their caretaker and at a remove from most of their culture seem to learn language faster if they are addressed with the tutorial adjustments of CDS, children being brought up in multi-person groups with more routinised cultural activities being carried out within their view seem to be hearing enough utterances which they can pair with meaning to learn to use language. Lieven argues that while cultures differ in the balance of strategies they use to induct children into language, there are some ways of doing it which are common to many cultures, for example teaching polite ways of talking. Others vary more between cultures, for example the naming games of CDS versus the use of names embedded in ordinary conversation about the world; or the use of "display" questions, where the adult knows the answer and the child knows the adult knows, versus questions for real new information and rhetorical effect. The very interesting ethnographic account of such differences provided by Heath (1983) suggests that these varying ways of allowing children into language may have different costs and different benefits. What these are may not be obvious until the child moves away from home to a new social setting: Western schooling, for example, depends heavily on language use that resembles the skills acquired from middle-class Western CDS, rather than those derived from experience of language embedded in the solidarity and familiarity of the social group.

This is an argument which can be extended to other aspects of adult–child interaction. Rogoff (1993) describes guided participation in cultural activity by toddlers and caregivers, the children and adults being drawn from middle-class suburbs in the USA and Turkey, and rural communities in Guatemala and India. She argues, as a cultural anthropologist, that guided participation is just one plane of analysis in the understanding of how people develop in sociocultural contexts; other important planes include processes of community change and of individual change. Processes on each plane need the background of other planes; the communities studied, for example, differed in where they were in the process of urbanisation with its attendant changes in community practices, such as schooling and work. Cultural practices on this plane make it easier or harder for children and adults to engage in different modes of guided participation; opportunities for observation and instruction differ according to the ongoing activities and the economic demands of the setting. Nevertheless, there were universals in guided participation between the toddlers and their adult partners. In all four communities, they collaborated in bridging between their individual understandings of the situations at hand, and in their structuring of each other's participation in activities, using both tacit and explicit forms of communication and direct hands-on arrangements of children's activities. Rogoff argues that these universals are inherent to the nature of shared activity, which cannot proceed without some degree of shared understanding and some mutual adjustment of involvement. She points out that this is as true of the interaction of children and others in routine cultural activities such as tending livestock or learning to weave, as it is in more formal, didactic, self-conscious settings. She sees the former as potentially just as relevant for the study of cognitive development as the latter, although it is the latter that psychologists interested in the role of adult–child interaction in cognitive development have focused on.

Rogoff also sees variations in the goals of development and the nature of involvement between child and adult between the four cultures studied. Cultures differ in the preferred metaphor for child development. Children are "coming up" in some cultures, and are "brought up" in others; although the direction "up" is common to both metaphors, in one children are doing it themselves and in the other a lot of parental effort is implied. Cultures differ in what exactly "upness" is for the child; being literate, for example, is important in some but not in others. They differ also in the age by which a certain degree of upness is expected, at the point in life by which one is weaned or becomes head of a household, for example, and in the rigidity with which this is required. Cultural goals are one source of the determinants of what a culture provides for its children's development.

Rogoff (1993, p. 151) suggests there are:

> two patterns for learning the mature roles of a community that appear to be accompanied by variation in whether children are allowed to observe and participate in ongoing adult activities. In communities where they are segregated from adult activities, children's learning may be organised by adults' teaching of lessons and provision of motivational management out of the context of adult practice; in communities in which children are integrated in adult settings, learning can occur through active observation and participation by the children with responsive assistance by caregivers ... In the two communities [Guatemala and India] in which children have the opportunity to observe and participate in adult social and work activities, caregivers appeared to support their toddlers' own efforts with responsive assistance, and toddlers appeared to take responsibility for observing ongoing events and beginning to enter adult activity. In the two communities in which children are usually segregated from adult activities [suburban Turkey and New England], caregivers seemed to take responsibility for organising children's involvement by managing their motivation and by instructing through the provision of lessons (especially in language use) and through play and conversation as peers with the toddlers.

Toddlers actually got less sensitive support and assistance during the period of observation in the latter, more Western communities, because their mothers' instruction and "scaffolding", while explicit in the recognisable teaching situation of helping the child explore a novel object, dropped off during situations which the mothers did not recognise as instructional, such as episodes of dressing and of the child exploring the novel object while the mother was attending to the researcher's questions. The mothers from Guatemala, however, non-middle-class and non-Western, contrastingly provided sensitive assistance to the children during all three sorts of activity, and their children remained alertly involved in the interaction, unlike the toddlers in the more Western settings who were more passive while being dressed, and operated on the novel toys without their mothers. Rogoff, like Heath, sees adult-constructed adult–child interaction as a preparation for participation in structurally and motivationally similar interactions in formal school; indeed, such a preparation is often an explicit goal of middle-class urban mothers in the West. The segregation of children (and their mothers) from many of the adult activities of the culture means that there are few opportunities for the children to learn through observing and participating in adult activities. In more traditional societies, where children are not segregated from adult activities, they have more opportunities to observe them, to participate in them and to become fully competent participants in them. Adults here have, perhaps, less need to organise specialised learning sessions for the children. More of the everyday activities that adults have to do are accessible to children, both in being done in their presence on a time-scale which allows adults to adjust their work fairly easily to their child's involvement, and in being perhaps easier to follow than the more fragmented practices of a Western assembly line or the mysterious operations of adult uses of literacy.

Rogoff (1993) found a difference between the apparent attentiveness of the Western and non-Western groups. In the latter, both adults and toddlers were able to share their attention among competing events, which both facilitated adult responsivity to the child's activities and enabled sensitive non-verbal help to be offered very rapidly to a child in need of it, and allowed the child to monitor a more complex and multi-peopled range of adults' behaviour. I find this particularly interesting, as the ability to share attention effectively between two activities was characteristic of the most competent children in two of my own studies of children in nursery and reception classes (Meadows & Cashdan, 1988; Meadows & Mills, 1987). The "well-functioning" children could both perform a task well and react very quickly to something in a way that showed they had been aware of it while working well on their focal task. For example, they could both build a Lego model and be part of a pretend discussion of an outer space adventure. Less well-functioning children might be able to devote their attention to one activity, giving up the other, or to alternate between them, but were much less likely to be able to do both at once. Children who were not functioning at all well tended either never to concentrate on anything (for one child aged 6 years her maximum period on any activity before she flitted off or switched to something else was 40 sec), or to appear to be so totally absorbed in something that there was no attention to spare for anything else; eyelids down, ear-lids down, shoulders hunched and the world excluded. How to attend effectively to the various stimulation that the world provides is one of the problems of cognitive development. How to cope with the noise and distraction of the classroom is one of the problems of life as a pupil.

Most of the work on adult–child interaction and children's cognitive development involves studies of biologically related parents and children, and hence is vulnerable to claims that any associations found are the results of genetic resemblances rather than of a more direct effect of parent behaviour on the child (see the discussion of recent work in developmental behaviour genetics below). One additional problem about assessing the effects of differences in parents' behaviour on children's cognitive development is that we have little detailed information on the naturally occurring day-to-day experience of small children in their normal settings. Most studies have used small samples, not necessarily representative of the whole population. The measuring instruments used have also varied. It is difficult to compare the results of studies which have used different samples, different measures and different variables as their focus. The problems of what to look for and how to assess it are so complex that there has been nothing like a comprehensive study of young children's experience.

Much useful material has been gathered using instruments such as the HOME inventory (Bradley 1994; Bradley & Caldwell, 1980, 1984; Bradley, Caldwell, & Rock, 1988; Bradley et al., 1989; Caldwell & Bradley, 1978; Gottfried & Gottfried, 1984; Luster & Dubow, 1992). The HOME Inventory includes assessments of mothers' responsivity, avoidance of restriction and punishment, organisation of the environment, play materials, maternal involvement in the child's activities, and opportunities for variety in daily stimulation. These variables intercorrelate positively but not perfectly, so levels of prediction from age to age are hard to interpret. However, the research data fairly consistently show low to moderate positive correlations between the amount of warm participation in socially and culturally stimulating interactions and the child's cognitive development, even when maternal IQ and educational level are partialled out in an attempt to control for passive genotype–environment interaction. Correlations between these measures and status on infant developmental scales during the first year are low, but HOME scores correlate more highly with assessments of intelligence and later school achievement as the child gets older, at least for the usual run of American and European samples, as evidence is lacking on whether other cultures may use different but functionally equivalent ways of supporting development. The measure has been less widely used with other samples, and the correlations may be lower (Bradley, 1994). The HOME Inventory is a complex instrument, and the data it provides do not show which aspects of what it scores are causal variables and which merely associates of a causal variable; but its assessment of the availability of age-appropriate play materials, the possibility of free visual and physical exploration of the environment, parental warmth and responsiveness, and involvement in joint play may provide indices of a pattern of interaction with adults which incorporates parental scaffolding and support for the child's desires and initiatives, and allows the child to develop both culturally valued skills and a sense of mastery. On the whole, research studies using the HOME Inventory or similar measurements agree with the developmental psychopathology literature, some of which I discuss in Chapter 6, that it is a bad thing to have very little of this sort of interaction, and within the samples studied there is very little to suggest that a child could have too much of it.

Studies which look at patterns of parent–child behaviour may explain associations between parent "input" and child "outcome", which can be dismissed as due to the genes they both share, as being correlates at different points in the life cycle of the genetic continuity which is the major causal variable (Rowe, 1994). Such a dismissal overlooks the point that although the genes may indeed programme both the parents' and the child's behaviour, they may also need the parents' behaviour as a direct cause of the child's. For example, in birds such as chaffinches which have elaborate songs, there is a genetic programme which leads the young males to produce a chaffinch song; but a young bird's earlier exposure to the local variant of this song is what determines its fine details (e.g. Macfarlane, 1987). Genes may be an ultimate cause but interaction may be an equally necessary proximal one. The next chapter addresses this issue. Meanwhile, this brief review of the literature on adult–child interaction and children's development suggests that there is an association between more "scaffolding" in interaction and better cognitive and language development in normal Western populations. However, there are problems. The association between more scaffolding and better cognitive and language development is quite weak, with correlations typically positive but low. Scaffolding is just one part of the cultural tool kit applied to bringing up children and to using language, and we do not know how it is associated with the use of other cultural tools—which might be the tools that are producing the effect we ascribe to scaffolding. We do not know about possible functional equivalents, either in our own culture or in other cultures. It is not clear what direction of effect there is, whether the adult scaffolder produces an effect in the child learner or whether the child controls the adult's behaviour. It seems to me to be necessary to look at alternative explanations, so the next chapter looks at two which place the cause of the association outside the interaction.

CHAPTER FIVE

Is the apparent effect of scaffolding an epiphenomenon?

INTRODUCTION

Chapter 3 presented the theoretical case for adult–child interaction as a major formative influence on cognitive development, and Chapter 4 described some of the relevant observational data. My task in this chapter is to address arguments that there is no significant causal link between parent–child interaction and the child's cognitive development, but rather that the association is due to the effects of a third, underlying variable. The major argument that has to be taken into account here is the current version of an old one, that the association between parent behaviour in the form of scaffolding and child outcome in the form of better cognitive development comes about because parent and child share genes for intelligence, which are expressed in the parenting behaviour of the adult on the one hand, and in the ability to learn of the child on the other. This case was made in pioneering studies of intelligence 100 or more years ago, such as Francis Galton's "Hereditary Genius"; the current, and more rigorous case, is being made by the developmental behaviour geneticists. It is their work that receives most attention in this chapter. But this argument for a cause of intelligence and cognitive development that is genetic, or innate, or "natural", has always been opposed by the argument that the cause is to be found in "nurture", an effect of acquired experience or of different social conditions. Work on differences between different social classes, and work looking at the effects of various environmental conditions, is the main source of data for this argument. Unlike the "intelligence is genetically determined" argument, the environmentalists would not dismiss adult–child interaction as a cause of cognitive development, but they would wish to locate it within a consideration of wider sociological variables such as access to education and employment, and to show more consciousness of the difficult socio-political issues that arise. This certainly has to be done, but I will do no more than outline a few relevant points here.

SOCIAL ADDRESS RESEARCH

In societies with little social mobility, and education reserved for a few social groups, the social class of origin of a child is an excellent predictor of that child's cognitive attainment. Although a few individuals from families with low socio-economic status (SES) may show outstanding achievement, they will be the exceptions; not many blacksmiths' sons managed to achieve what Michael Faraday did, nor many farm labourers produce poems like John Clare's. Part of the impulse behind reformers working for universal access to education was a sense that there was unfulfilled cognitive potential in the lower social classes (and among women) that could only be realised if they were educated. Education is generally regarded as a means to cognitive achievement and to social mobility, as well as (or perhaps rather than) a good in itself.

Societies which are egalitarian or meritocratic, and which have a high degree of individual mobility, will show less association between social class of origin and the educational achievement of the child. Many people in countries like Britain and the United States believe that their society is of this sort, and there certainly is more equality of opportunity than there was in the days of Galton. However, despite more than 100 years of compulsory education in Britain, there are still social class differences in educational achievement and possibly in cognition more generally. Children from more middle-class backgrounds or with more educated parents still do better throughout their educational careers, staying in education longer and having higher achievement at most stages. They also tend to do better on IQ tests, in particular contributing relatively few cases to the population of marginally subnormal scorers. The SES of the family is still a fairly good predictor of children's academic achievement in most countries (Blake, 1989; Jencks, 1975; Marjoribanks, 1979, 1994; Rutter, 1985, 1992; Schaffer, 1992). It is not, incidentally, a good predictor of infant intelligence (Slater, 1995). This may be because the association between later IQ and SES is due to the accumulated social experience of the child, and more than a year or two of experience is needed to show an effect of class differences in interaction and opportunity; or because of methodological problems of sampling or testing; or because of conceptual problems to do with what is included in assessments. There is not yet enough evidence to evaluate these possibilities. However, we cannot at present discard the hypothesis that I would favour, that there are no significant class differences in the intelligence of infants beyond those with a medical cause, and that later IQ differences are the result of experiences associated with social class.

Socio-economic status in itself is not a causal variable. It is typically an index of the father's occupation, and hence of the family's income, the parents' education and, less directly, their housing, health, etc. It is what Bronfenbrenner (1979, 1986) calls a "social address"—a correlated measure rather than an explanatory variable. Eysenck (1971) argued that it is an index of people's innate intelligence, on the dubious grounds of his belief that social mobility has been easy enough for long enough that no-one would be left in a low social class now unless they were too ineradicably stupid to rise above it. More plausibly than this unsavoury victim-blaming, it could be that the remaining social class differences in access to good health care might lead to less than optimum prenatal brain development and later health; worse housing, diet and health care lead to poorer physical development and both major and minor illnesses which interrupt both formal and informal educational processes (Meadows, 1993, pp. 294–302). Relative poverty may also lead directly to worse educational opportunities. For example, there may be differences in per capita expenditure in publicly funded and private schools, or between schools in richer and poorer areas; opportunities to do homework or read around a subject will be restricted if the family cannot provide quiet study space or access to relevant material; staying on in the education system will be harder if the child has to begin to contribute to the family economically at an early age. Significant other people may react differently to children from different backgrounds, expecting more or less achievement and so evoking it differently from privileged and disadvantaged children. At present there is no research which would allow any of these possible causes of class differences to be ruled out or identified as especially important. My own belief is that the more social causes of these differences are more plausible than unalterable innate differences. Three main sets of evidence support this view. First, adoption studies (see below) do show a change in IQ scores for children adopted into a social class different from that of their birth parents; French studies (Capron & Duyme, 1989; Duyme, 1988; Schiff & Lewontin, 1986; see also Scarr & Weinberg, 1983; Seglow,

Kellmer-Pringle, & Wedge, 1972; Tizard, 1977) show an exactly parallel shift in educational careers too. Second, epidemiological studies, such as the very large Collaborative Perinatal Project in the United States (Broman, Nichols, Shaughnessy, & Kennedy, 1987), find that although severe cognitive deficit is spread across all social classes, mild retardation is much more closely linked to SES, being very rare in high SES groups, and more common in blacks than in whites. In the main, severe mental retardation has clear medical causes in central nervous system (CNS) damage; mild retardation is only weakly associated with any medical indices during the early years, especially among black children, who often seem to have been quite normal in all their early measures while performing at a low level on IQ tests at seven or older. Third, the intriguing secular shift in IQ, which (if evidence from more than a dozen countries is to be trusted) has risen 12–15 points over the last 30–40 years (Flynn, 1987; Lynn, 1993), suggests both environmental influences on IQ (because this is too short a period for genetic change) and specifically an educational effect, because educational opportunities and expectations have clearly risen over this period, and so has educational achievement, though this is harder to measure accurately. Some researchers argue that the important historical change has been in health rather than education. There have indeed been changes in medical practice (e.g. fewer forceps deliveries that may have caused some brain damage and so some mental retardation); however, there have also been changes in doctors' ability to keep very preterm and low birthweight babies alive, with the consequence that many more survive but with some brain damage that affects their cognitive performance (Cooke, 1994; Escobar, Littenberg, & Pettiti, 1991; Johnson et al., 1993). Changes in diet, which are hard to document precisely, may have tended towards better nutritional status, and nutritional status is certainly important for brain development and cognition, though the causal pathways are complex (see Meadows, 1993; Puckering et al., 1995); or the changing diet may have included too much "junk food" and additives with unknown effects on brain development and functioning. The secular trend of an increase in height, which began late last century, has slowed considerably, so the increased physical fitness of the population may or may not be real. Pollution from traffic fumes has certainly increased since the 1950s and 1960s, and would have tended to reduce cognitive performance through the CNS damage that lead poisoning causes, and through illnesses such as asthma and their interruption of schooling.

There is still, then, an association between class and achievement. While there are many differences between classes that may be contributing to this, are there grounds for implicating interaction differences as a cause, rather than the other associates of social address? The studies of language development and of literacy discussed earlier, particularly those of Wells (1985) and Snow (1995), provide some evidence that this could be the case, though not enough to establish it firmly. One further body of evidence on the "social address" front helps my case for interaction as a cause of cognitive development. A recent American study (Blake, 1989) provides a rigorous scrutiny of several large sets of data to examine the links between family size and achievement. Blake finds a consistent difference in total educational attainment between the offspring of large and small families. Those from large families are less likely to get through grade school without being kept down a grade, to complete high school, to have high verbal IQ scores, or to have high educational goals. Their achievement is more closely constrained by their social origins, they have less confidence in their abilities than those abilities would justify, and they are more likely to underperform in school relative to their ability scores. These differences between large and small families are found throughout the range of social groups, though they are reduced somewhat by such other social forces as high parental SES, a cultural emphasis on educational attainment, or an exceptionally cohesive kin network.

Blake argues that the cause of this difference in cognitive achievement between sib-size groups is that parents' efforts to support their children's cognition are a crucial factor in its development, and that these parental efforts are "diluted" if they have to be spread over many children. She cites various pieces of evidence for this explanation: the advantage in verbal IQ but not in non-verbal IQ for children from small families, which suggests parental attention and conversation as a cause; the increased amounts of time that children from small families spent at home engaged in intellectual and cultural pursuits and in playing alone, and the greater frequency of being read to that they report they enjoyed as preschoolers; the decrease in the sib-size effect in families from social groups which foster educational achievement. It is also relevant that it is the middle-born children from large families close in age who tend to do worst; unlike their older and younger siblings, they have never been the only child on whom their parents' educative attentions could be focused, but have always had to share them with their sibs. We can only speculate, unfortunately, about exactly how interaction with parents differed for these children; but perhaps there was less interaction with parents, less that focused on an object or activity demanding and receiving joint attention, less child-contingent and responsive interaction, less enthusiasm, more interruption, less success and confidence, a reduced expectation of what could be achieved, both now and in the future.

Thus, "social address" variables such as social class remain cheap and not ineffective indices of probable educational achievement. This is probably not because of innate differences in the intelligence and cognition of different social classes, but because of differences in their "cultural capital", for example their access to educational opportunities. Differences which begin to appear in the preschool years, and differences between large and small families, are consistent with an effect of parent–child scaffolding on children's cognitive development.

DEVELOPMENTAL BEHAVIOUR GENETICS

"Social address" research suggests a link between characteristics of families and cognitive outcomes for children, perhaps partly brought about by the nature of adult–child interaction within families. But we must now look at a recent argument which could on the face of it have a devastating effect on any search for the influence of environmental factors such as adult–child interaction on children's cognitive development. Developmental behaviour geneticists, among them Sandra Scarr, Robert Plomin and Thomas Bouchard, are making a case that siblings do not resemble each other particularly closely, that what resemblance there is is genetic, that shared environmental factors such as parents' level of education do not have any significant long-term effects on personality or intelligence, and that the most important environmental factors are not shared by siblings. This line of argument suggests that the parent–child interaction that is the favourite candidate of neo-Vygotskians cannot be so influential as they would suppose, unless it is unevenly distributed across the children within a family rather than being the parents' habitual style.

Developmental behaviour genetics arouses strong and partisan reactions (e.g. Baumrind, 1993; Jackson, 1993; Scarr, 1992; see also Alper & Natowicz, 1992; Byne, 1994; Maddox, 1993) because of its relevance to the "nature–nurture" argument, which has done so much damage to psychology—and to social policy and to some vulnerable individuals, as Gould (1984) describes. The dichotomising of "nature" and "nurture" obscures rather than elucidates their interplay in development. There can be no dispute that both genes and environment are necessary for development. Developmental behaviour geneticists do on the whole recognise this, though lapses into brash apparent dismissals of environmental influences such as that by Rowe (1994) are not difficult to find. Part of the importance of their work is indeed the evidence it provides for the importance of variance, which is definitely environmental rather than genetic. However, the case I have made for effects of adult–child interaction on cognitive development looks different from their position, which would include suggestions that this "environmental" variation has a genetic basis and that any "effects" largely vanish in adolescence and adulthood.

The main methods used in developmental behaviour genetics are familiar (in both the senses of that word); twin, family (both intact two-parent and step families) and adoption studies. These studies take a large population and attempt to break down the variation in a characteristic that the population shows into genetic and environmental components. While most of the genetic material is the same from one individual to another, indeed from one mammal to another, people born into the same family (e.g. parents and children, or siblings) resemble each other in the genes that do vary between individuals; on average, parents and children, or siblings, share 50% of these. More distant relations share genes to a lesser extent. Identical twins share all their genes. If related people do not resemble each other on a trait any more than the general population, then their genetic similarity (and their shared environment) cannot be of great importance for their similarity on that trait. If they do resemble each other more closely, then resemblance on the trait may be due to their shared genes; or to the environment which they also share; or to both. Studies of biologically related people who live together and share their environments cannot separate genetic and environmental influences; thus they cannot successfully attribute the trait to any genetic or environmental influence. Twin and adoption studies help to clarify these possible influences. Identical twins are genetically identical, and fraternal twins are 50% identical on average. They probably share the same environment to about the same degree (if we confine our argument to same-sex fraternal twins). If hereditary transmission contributes to family resemblance, then identical twins should be more alike than fraternal twins because they share more genetic material; if it does not, they will resemble each other to much the same extent. "Heritability", the effect size of genetic influence, can be estimated by comparing the similarities between differently related pairs of people.

While twin studies seek to control environmental variation to examine the importance of genes, adoption studies can compare genetically unrelated people who have been adopted into, and brought up in, the same family environment (assuming, for the moment, that adoptive families are like non-adoptive ones). If genetic factors are all-important, these unrelated individuals will not be particularly alike; if the shared environment of rearing is important, they will resemble each other. The correlation between unrelated people living together is an estimate of the effect of their shared environment.

The main strategy of the developmental behaviour geneticists is to compare correlations between different pairs of family members and use model-fitting to assess the relative importance of genetic and environmental influences. The strategy is obviously dependent on good (and large) samples, good measures, and correct assumptions about various confounding variables such as assortative mating (people's tendency to seek out similar but unrelated people as spouses), non-additive genetic variance, such as dominant genes, and selective placement of adoptive children. It also depends on twins being developmentally the same as singletons, and adopted children the same as non-adopted ones, if extrapolations are to be made to the majority of the population.

Height provides a clear and uncontroversial example. The correlations for height between parent and child, between fraternal twins, and between ordinary siblings are all about 0.45, whether they live together or are adopted apart; the correlation between identical twins is about 0.90. This pattern of correlations suggests a strong genetic influence on height; in fact, about 90% of the variance in height in the populations studied is due to genetic differences. Environmental factors do contribute to the variance of these populations, but to a much smaller extent. They influence the average for the population, but they do not have much effect on family resemblance. Improvements in health and nutrition have increased the height of most Western populations over the last 100 years, but they have not made it possible for parents who are small compared with other parents to have children who are tall compared with other children. The "secular trend" in height has applied, presumably, to all those who received the better environment, and increased their heights by about the same proportion.

This point, that genetic studies of this sort are concerned with resemblances and differences amongst siblings and other family members, and not about absolute scores on tests or on traits, is important. It will be part of my defence of the need to continue to look at shared environmental influences. It is also important to remember that estimates of genetic variance apply only to the populations studied within the environments they have experienced; if the population is changed or the environment changes, the pattern of genetic and environmental influence may change too. Genetic variability and selection always operate within environments, just as environments always operate on genetic variability. Evolutionary theory asserts the importance of genetic variability continuing to exist in the gene pool so that future variability in environmental challenges can be met.

In the sense in which behaviour geneticists use it, "heritability" means something more precise than "capable of being inherited", which is the ordinary dictionary definition. Within a population, a trait varies over a certain range. This variance can be partitioned into a component due to relevant genetic differences within the population, a component due to environmental differences, and a component due to the interaction of genetic and environmental differences. (There will also be some error variance, for example due to measurement problems.) If the trait in question were observed hair colour, say, some variation would be due to genetic differences of blackness, brownness, blondeness and so forth, some to environmental differences such as nutrition or exposure to sunlight or artificial bleaches and colourings, and some to cases of gene–environment interaction, as when the girl with naturally mousy hair realises that her skin colour naturally "goes" with a restricted range of mid-brown and russet, and gives up fantasies of being an ash-blonde or a Titian-haired beauty in favour of less extreme though still artificially aided shades. Heritability is, at its broadest, the proportion of population variance which is due to genetic differences; in most developmental behaviour genetic studies it is, more narrowly, that part of the entire genetic component which is due to additive genetic differences between individuals. It may be seen that what proportion of the variation is heritable is affected by how much environmental variation there is (and vice versa); if the environment does not allow the opportunity of changing the colour of your hair, for example, then variation in hair colour will be much more closely associated with genetic variation than if bleaches and dyes are available and socially sanctioned. This means that estimates of heritability derived from one population with a particular range of environments might not be an appropriate estimate for a population with different environments, or indeed for a genetically different population. The heritability of hair colour among 9-year-olds will be higher than the heritability of hair colour among 18-year-olds, because the former have less access to environmental influences than the latter, where fashion, self-assertion, financial control and a spirit of *il faut épater les bourgeois* (especially parents) have all increased and may make the use of artificial hair colourings more likely. This point about the reciprocal nature of the "genetic" and "environmental" components of population variance is another important one to bear in mind; this, too, will enter into my discussion of adult–child interaction and cognitive development.

Furthermore, even if a trait is strongly heritable, that does not mean that "environmental" influences are not important or that it cannot be environmentally modified. There will still be environmental influences on how the genetic programme proceeds. The genetic defect of phenylketonuria provides a good example. Phenylketonuria is due to a single defective gene that causes a failure to produce the enzyme phenylhydroxylase, required to metabolise phenylalanine, which is ingested from protein in most ordinary human diets. This metabolic problem causes an accumulation of unmetabolised phenylalanine, which swamps the developing nervous system, damaging brain cell processes, and hence mental retardation results. Since the genetic defect can be identified at birth and a diet which does not contain phenylalanine can be provided, it is possible to get round the metabolic deficiency, prevent the nervous system from being damaged and reduce the mental retardation to a minimal amount. The gene which causes phenylketonuria is still inherited, but provided people with that gene have an environment free of phenylalanine while their brains are developing (and while, if they are pregnant women, their babies' brains are developing), the gene will not affect the trait of intelligence.

Given these warnings about the meaning of heritability and the methodological problems of the area, what do the developmental behaviour genetics studies say about parent–child resemblances in cognition? The evidence from a number of recent large-scale studies of twins (see Tables 5.1 and 5.2 below) suggests that the heritabilities of five major personality dimensions (extraversion, neuroticism, agreeableness, conscientious- ness and openness to experience), are between 0.40 and 0.50 (Bouchard, 1994; Loehlin, 1992; Plomin, 1994b, 1995). Estimates of the heritability of IQ suggest a similar figure, though perhaps there is some evidence for an effect of shared environment (McGue, 1994). Genetic resemblance seems to be leading to a noteworthy degree of similarity between related individuals so far as their personality and intelligence are concerned. This is interesting but not especially surprising. The next question is, does shared family environment add to this?

TABLE 5.1

Heritability of personality: Model-fitting meta-analysis of twin and adoption studies of the "big five" personality dimensions

	Heritability (additive genetic effect)	Special monozygotic twin effect (non-additive genetic effect or special mono-zygotic environment effect)
Extraversion	0.36	0.16
Neuroticism	0.31	0.16
Agreeableness	0.28	0.15
Conscientiousness	0.28	0.17
Openness to experience[a]	0.46	0.04

[a] From Plomin (1994a, p. 821).

TABLE 5.2
Twin results for studies of behavioural disorders and dimensions

	Identical twins	Fraternal twins
Twin correlations		
Personality	0.50	0.20
MMPI	0.45	0.20
Childhood behaviour problems	0.80	0.60
Vocational interests	0.50	0.25
Social attitudes	0.65	0.50
IQ	0.85	0.60
Twin concordances		
Conduct disorder	0.85	0.70
Alcoholism – males	0.40	0.20
Alcoholism – females	0.30	0.25
Schizophrenia	0.40	0.10
Unipolar depression	0.45	0.20
Manic depression	0.65	0.20
Autism [a]	0.65	0.10

[a] From Plomin (1994a, p. 821).

The answer put forward by the developmental behaviour geneticists is that it adds very little if anything; indeed, that for personality there may be all sorts of almost deliberate attempts to become different from one's sib (Hartup & van Lieshout, 1995; Hoffman, 1991; Reiss et al., 1994). As intelligence must to a certain extent be heritable, resemblances between biologically related parents and children might be attributed to heredity rather than to shared environment. The best evidence on shared environment and intelligence therefore comes from adoption studies. If the shared family environment affects unrelated children brought together in the adoptive family, then they should resemble each other. If they do not resemble each other more than the general population, the case for the effect of the shared family environment is weakened.

One major source of data is the Colorado Adoption Project (CAP). This well-documented study (DeFries, Plomin, & Fulker, 1994; Plomin & DeFries, 1985; Plomin, DeFries, & Fulker, 1988) began in 1974 as a longitudinal prospective study of the development of behaviour in adopted and non-adopted children, with measures of parents' and children's abilities and of the environment being taken at frequent intervals throughout infancy, childhood and adolescence. It has examined the degree of resemblance between children and their adoptive or non-adoptive parents and siblings; it has also looked at genetic change and continuity. One focus has been the role of the shared and the non-shared environment. During childhood, adopted brothers and sisters do resemble each other in intelligence, but the correlation in adolescent or adult samples in other studies (as CAP data from these ages are not yet available) is much lower, suggesting no resemblance and thus no lasting effect of the shared environment. By this time, Plomin and his colleagues believe, non-shared environmental influences have had time to work. There may be some problems here in that their adopted children are mostly in opposite sex pairs, and of different ages (Cherny & Cardon, 1994), and therefore the CAP analyses cannot easily detect environmental effects shared by siblings of the same sex or age; but the finding of low resembance between adopted siblings and thus of a lack of effect of their shared environment is intriguing.

This distinction between shared and non-shared environmental influences is a new and very important one. Shared environmental influences are those which tend to make those experiencing them more similar; their effect can be estimated from adoption studies or from the extent to which resemblance between identical twins is greater than that due to shared genes (calculated specifically as the identical twin correlation minus heritability). Non-shared environmental influences are those which do not contribute to family resemblance; their effect is estimated from how much variance is left after components due to genetic influence and shared environmental influence have been calculated. This residual variance is due to non-shared environment, non-shared genes and errors of measurement. Each of these components can be estimated, though the whole network of calculations is too complex to be set out here. (There are also some queries about the mathematical models used, for example about the assumption of additive genetic effects predominating, and about the assessment of environment from residual variance.)

The ineffectiveness of the shared environment in Plomin's and Bouchard's samples is an extremely interesting finding. It is in particular surprising that they find so little resemblance between unrelated children reared together in adopted and step families. There are, however, some important caveats to be made about their work. First, as mentioned earlier, all estimates of the relative influence of genetic and environmental factors are specific to the particular combination of genetic range and environmental range studied. The samples used would appear to be predominantly white, middle-class, well-off Americans (Bouchard, 1994; Plomin, 1994b). In the case of the

CAP they are "representative of the Denver metropolitan area in terms of socio-economic status ... similar both in means and variances to a stratified random sample from a Denver suburban area taken from the 1970 census data ... somewhat above the national average in occupational status ..." (DeFries et al., 1994, p. 13) and almost all white. Bouchard (1994) describes a sample which also seems to be comparatively well-off and well-educated, though the ranges and standard deviations are not presented, nor is a clear comparison with the national average provided. The bulk of the behaviour genetics evidence comes from samples in which there seem to be no very disadvantaged families; all were prosperous working-class or middle-class, and had consented to stay in the sample over a long period. All the samples have also had access to a universal state education system. The environment and particularly the educational environment for samples like these would probably be fairly similar from family to family. Bouchard and Scarr recognise that their data cannot show whether there may be a shared environment effect from rearing under particularly disadvantageous circumstances because all the environments enjoyed by their samples were at least averagely advantaged, but their acknowledgement of this point is perhaps a little grudging. Baumrind (1993) and Jackson (1993) take Scarr (1992) to task for talking as if her sample was representative of the American population as a whole, as if in the United States all children benefited from what Scarr incautiously called the expectable good-enough environment. It is important to consider whether one's samples are really representative of the species, if one wishes to make claims about species-wide development. But it is perhaps even more important to recognise that it is impossible to discover an environmental effect if environmental variance is severely reduced. A uniform rather good environment might have uniform rather good effects on almost all those who enjoyed it; the only major source of differences between them would not be environmental. It would be hard to see the universal environmental effects, especially if the research strategy was to examine individual differences within a uniform environment. Studies of more extreme environments will be very useful in clarifying how much intelligence is affected by environments. They may also help to show how the environmental effects come about. I discuss studies of this sort in the next chapter.

Second, the outcome measures have to be appropriate and sensitive, and also properly conceptualised. The main measure of cognitive development reported in some studies is IQ, with educational achievement less frequently included. Little is said about the reliability and validity of IQ. Although studies such as Bouchard's and Plomin's do report their measures properly, it is not always certain that a full-scale and reputable test has been administered in other studies; to do so to hundreds or even thousands of subjects would be enormously expensive, and age differences within samples mean that there are real problems of comparability. IQ measures have always, moreover, sought to provide a measurement of intelligence as an "innate, general cognitive ability" uncontaminated by education. If they have succeeded in this, they have by definition excluded measures which are sensitive to environmental influences. Studies which use other measures in addition to IQ may be more useful, if only by showing the low to moderate correlations between measures. Longitudinal studies (Cardon, 1994; Cardon, Fulker, DeFries, & Plomin, 1992; Loehlin, 1987; McCartney, Harris, & Bernieri, 1990; Neiderhiser, 1994; Rose, 1995; Thompson, 1993) can show the extent of continuities and changes in environmental influences and heritability, and in the correlations between measures, during development. There will have to be careful consideration of issues such as the comparability of tests, their reliability, the results of floor effects and ceiling effects, and possible confounding variables, before interpretations are made. Similarly, it will be necessary to think very carefully about how one variable might relate to another conceptually as well as quantitatively, if causal sequences are to be understood adequately.

Rutter, Silberg and Simonoff (1994) make important points about measurements and samples. They argue that most of the measurements used so far have been comparatively crude, and make a case for multi-method assessment, multi-occasion measurement, and the study of constellations of behaviour rather than single scores. They emphasise the interest and importance of variations with age in developmental studies. They also point out that there has not been enough research into the differences between twins and singletons, and between monozygotic and dizygotic twins. Twins are unlike single births in their prenatal experience, their need for obstetric care, their birthweights, their mother's age, and so forth. Similar points about the differences between adopted and non-adopted children, and between children in different family circumstances, will also complicate the results of developmental behaviour genetics studies using adopted, step and non-adoptive intact families. As an example, it appears (Rose, 1995) that parents' ratings of the personalities of dizygotic twins may systematically emphasise their differences. The correlation between ratings of dizygotic twins by parents is much lower than that between monozygotic twins, though teachers and independent observers rate both sorts of twins as equally similar. There may be a similar problem with twins' ratings of themselves. This complicates the use of ratings by family members in the assessment of twin similarities and differences—whose ratings are "accurate"?

There is controversy in this area about the adequacy of the statistical analyses used in many studies (e.g. Baumrind, 1993; Jackson, 1993; Plomin, 1994b, 1995; Scarr, 1992, 1993), though it is beyond the aims of this essay to go into these except to say that adequate samples, proper measures, clear and appropriate analyses, and models which do not make incorrect or self-confirming assumptions, are essential.

In deciding on both samples and measures, it may be useful to remember the distinction I have already mentioned between "experience-expectant" and "experience-dependent" development and characteristics. It is clear that there are many important psychological functions which develop in all genetically normal individuals and in all normal environments, and that they are not very variable. Almost all intact human beings learn to use the full syntactic and phonetic range that their language uses unless they suffer extremes of deprivation; almost all intact human beings learn to hop, skip and jump. It appears that we possess the potential for these developments, and realising them requires only an almost universally available opportunity. The developmental process utilises the sort of environmental information that has been ubiquitous throughout the development of the species and can be relied on to occur in any individual's experience. This is "experience-expectant" development; the genes can safely, as it were, "expect" an adequately supportive environment. Variation in the environment is normally very limited, and will only lead to fine-tuning differences in development. "Experience-dependent" development is more variable. Only if appropriate environmental input is available will the genetically programmed development proceed—and the course of development will be dependent on the detail of the environment. Hopping, skipping and jumping are human universals; cricket is not, and nor is hopping, skipping and jumping at Olympic level. Syntax may be experience-expectant, vocabulary and the composition of poetry are much less so. There is some evidence for more shared environmental effects on specific cognitive abilities from the age of about nine (McGue, 1994; Plomin & McClearn, 1993; Rose, 1995), which may reflect the children's acquisition and use of literacy. Shared environment ("lifestyle") may be implicated here.

There is an analogous distinction between genes which make a species-specific but species-wide contribution and genes which differ among the parents and so differ among the offspring. Developmental behaviour genetics looks only at the second of these, because it is primarily concerned with individual differences. Focusing on individual differences is a necessary corrective to an exclusive focus on universals, but will not help us directly to understand universal processes. The techniques of molecular genetics, which identifies particular sequences of DNA associated with both defects and normal development, may be more illuminating here.

Interpreting a gene–behaviour association as being due to a specific gene with a strong predetermining influence is a temptation which the media and the general public frequently succumb to, and which is not always resisted by developmental behaviour geneticists. Plomin, for example, has described a genetic basis to differences in time spent watching TV (Plomin et al., 1990). As TV has only been available for about 40 years, there cannot possibly be a gene "for watching TV": the causal pathway between gene and behaviour is unclear but it must certainly be indirect. Without a great deal of further careful measurement and analysis, the association which has been found is meaningless.

There are problems, too, about the attribution of all of the similarity between related persons to genetic similarity, with a discounting of the shared environment of related persons as effective because it is seen as being caused by the shared genes. This must be too simple. If the argument is (and it must be) that shared genes programme a shared range of developmental potential and so produce a somewhat shared phenotype, then throughout development that phenotype must encounter and evoke environments which will also tend to be shared because of the powerful force of gene–environment interaction. The developmental behaviour geneticists (e.g. Bergeman & Plomin, 1988, 1989; Plomin, 1994b, 1995; Plomin & Bergeman, 1991; Plomin, Owen, & McGuffin, 1994a; Plomin, Reiss, Hetherington, & Howe, 1994b) correctly point out how the genetically influenced characteristics of a parent and child lead them to behave in particular ways, which are then assessed by such measures of "the environment" as the mother's responsivity or frequency with which books are read to the child. It is indeed an important point both that it is probably this sort of level of "environmental" measure that is most predictive of outcomes for the child, and that these measures are not free of influence from the characteristics of the child and the parent, characteristics that may have a genetic basis. But they are nevertheless truly environmental, in the sense that they exist outside the child's genotype. Furthermore, the converse applies; the shared environments will also affect how the shared genotype expresses itself in the future development of the phenotype. This means that you cannot partition population variance into a genetic component and an environmental component and stop there. In the model-fitting model for estimating the relative component of each, there has to be one or more interactional components.

In fact, the most interesting questions are about how different developmental influences interact. We know almost nothing about the interrelation of genes and environment, except that they operate together from conception on, so that even neonates have developed differences in brain cells due to the modulation of their genetic programmes for brain development under the influence of stimulation which they have experienced within the womb (Edelman, 1994). Monozygotic twins who became separate individuals early in development seem to be less alike than twins who separated later and shared a single placenta (Rose, 1995). The potential complexity of gene–environment interaction would seem, therefore, to begin at conception and to be enormous.

Scarr and McCartney (1983) described various possibilities of post-natal gene–environment covariation: "passive" covariance, where the child inherits both his or her parents' genes and the environment which the parents have set up because of their own genetically caused characteristics and preferences; "reactive" covariance, where other people provide the child with the environment that seems to them to fit his or her perceived phenotype; and "active" covariance, where the child seeks out environments which suit his or her phenotype. Thus, as well as the comparatively straightforward transmission of a characteristic to the child through inheritance of the relevant genes from the parent (and this may turn out not to be straightforward at all, as we do not know much yet about how most genes lead to particular characteristics), there will be indirect effects. There may be "passive" interaction between genotype and environment, where genetically related people provide an environment correlated with the child's own genes, as when the child with a genotype which would tend to lead to high intelligence is also surrounded by the intellectual pursuits and possessions of highly intelligent parents and siblings. There may be a "reactive" correlation, where the child's own phenotype may evoke responses from other people which are related to the child's characteristics, so the child's interest in books may be fostered by adults, or boys and girls may be provided with "sex-appropriate" toys. There may be "active" correlation, where the child seeks out environments which are comfortable for his or her phenotype, maximising the impact of congenial bits of the environment and minimising the less genotypically suitable bits as far as possible. Probably all of these sorts of interaction will occur; Scarr perhaps tends to overemphasise "active" correlation, "environmental niche picking", which may be a luxury more accessible to the late twentieth-century, middle-class, white Americans of the developmental behaviour genetics studies than it has been to the rest of the human race. Scarr and McCartney (1983) make the interesting point that the relative importance of different sorts of gene–environment correlation will change with age. The influence of passive correlation is greatest during infancy, and declines as the child's individuality becomes more recognisable and his or her opportunities for selecting experiences increase. Reactive effects continue throughout life, though not necessarily remaining the same throughout life, while active effects increase from infancy to adolescence as the child encounters successively wider environments with more variation to select from. This suggests that siblings will be more similar as young children, when passive genotype–environment effects dominate and they share the same environment, than they are as adolescents, when their experience varies more and more and they may even be seeking to be as different from each other as possible. The decrease in the correlation of siblings' IQ from childhood to adolescence would support this idea.

It is not difficult to think of examples of gene–environment interaction, but there is little in the way of documentation or measurement of such covariance within the developmental behaviour genetics literature (Bergeman & Plomin, 1988, 1989). A few, more clearly described examples can be found in research on environmental variation and children's characteristics, for example in the ways in which innate deafness or Down's syndrome affect adults' interaction with young children, and in some classroom observation literature on teachers' interaction with different children. I will discuss some of this evidence below.

We are similarly ignorant about gene–environment interaction in the sense of the non-linear impact of genetic and environmental influences on development. Most research designs look for linear relationships between one (or a few) variables and an outcome measure. It is technically much harder to find non-linear interaction between variables, but it seems likely that such interaction is often developmentally important. Risk factors, for example, may singly increase the risk of pathological development by a small amount, but in combination increase risk by far more than their sum as individual factors. Conversely, one factor may "buffer" development that would otherwise be made problematic by the presence of a risk factor. The development of children with Down's syndrome (Carr, 1988) provides examples of both (and illustrates the point that a variable can be both a risk factor and a buffer). There are consistent sub-group differences in the cognitive development of Down's children: girls do better than boys at both IQ tests and educational tests; home-raised children do better than those reared away from home on verbal ability, reading-level and arithmetic tests, but not on IQ tests; and non-manual SES children do significantly better than manual SES children on language and arithmetic tests, reading accuracy and reading-level scores, and non-significantly better on reading comprehension despite not having a higher IQ. Carr attributes this to the "resilience and courage" of the parents, who were transforming the unpromising genotype into a phenotype that enabled the children to lead much more satisfactory lives than their anomalous chromosomes would otherwise have allowed. Although it is possible that finer-grained genetic assessment of the chromosomal anomaly in Down's children might better predict their development, and some children are likely to be more resilient (or less vulnerable) than others, the differences in outcome, with the probable exception of the sex differences, are better predicted by the environmental input that parents and other caregivers provide, than by assessments of the children's genetic potential made at the outset.

The developmental behaviour geneticists are right to argue that the environmental variation has a genetic root, but it is nonetheless environmental variation, out there in the real social and physical world, not embodied in the genes. What is happening in the child's environment may have a genetic root which is making a causal contribution to the child's development, but the proximal cause is the environmental event. The identical genetic origin might lead to quite different outcomes if the proximal environment was different. Even if your genotype affects what environment you encounter—and it obviously does—there are still important questions to be asked about how each environment works. It is to be hoped that the developmental behaviour geneticists will contribute to this research. Although we all tend to see the first cause as the most important, and we try to trace back a causal sequence to the earliest identifiable step, we need to see how each step led to the next and how inevitable or avoidable this progress was. Until the whole sequence is understood, we will not know whether the first step was the critical one or whether it merely somehow made some much later event a little more likely to occur.

What are the merits at present of the behaviour geneticists' work? First, they finally slay the strong environmentalism that denied even minimal importance of the genes for behaviour. No-one could now deny that genes affect development and behaviour, and assert that the developmental range is entirely open and only environment has any effect. Environments must operate on a specific genetic potential. But similarly genes operate within the limits and potential of the environment.

Second, they draw attention to the importance and the difficulty of defining environments and measuring their effects. It has been difficult even to begin to systematise this (Bradley & Caldwell, 1995). The nearest approximation there is to a standard measure is the HOME inventory, with all its limitations (Bradley, 1994, provides a very useful review); there is no agreement on how to "parse" environments into significant units and systems; and attempts to manipulate environmental variables have often been ill-conceived, partial or temporary. Nevertheless, there is a vast array of both theory and usable data. What the developmental geneticists add to the need for a better understanding of both shared and non-shared environments is the importance of studying more than one child per family. Within-family variance is interesting in its own right and as a window on both genetic and environmental causes of variation.

Third, through their interest in families and the striking differences between siblings which they attribute to their emotional conflicts and personality clashes, they have reminded us of the importance of relationships and of emotion in the development of cognition and educational achievement. I have made a case elsewhere (Meadows, 1993) for thinking of cognition as "hot" not cold; again, there will be further discussion of this later.

Fourth, this controversy brings home to us the fascination and difficulty of bringing together phenomena and explanations derived from different research traditions and disciplines. In the case of population variance in intelligence, differences in genes may be an important ultimate cause, but more proximal ones are also crucial; I think the most exciting point here is about how the genetic programme is enacted within environments over time. We need to know the intricate causal sequences by which the DNA codes lead to protein syntheses, brain growth, curiosity levels, reasoning power, attractiveness as a pupil, and all the other interplaying behaviours, processes and structures which intervene between the genetic potential and the phenotypic realisation. Even such an impromptu list as this one shows what a challenge this is going to be!

Fifth, the controversy is a reminder of the interdependence of scientists and the wider society. All of us in our attempts to be scientists are continually influenced by many of our own social understandings, which are not scientific at all; furthermore, our research is read, interpreted and used by people with a non-scientific agenda. Our position as moral beings gives us the responsibility to do our research as properly as we can, to restrict our interpretations to what the data will bear, to guard against misinterpretations of our findings, to recognise that the questions we ask are not free of values and that our choice of what to ask and what to ignore is not neutral either, and to take responsibility for our actions both as scientists and as moral persons. If, for example, massive action to improve children's cognition led only to a small improvement, but no action at all led to no improvement at all, then one might be morally obliged to take the massive action rather than none at all.

It is important for psychologists who are interested in environmental effects to acknowledge fully the importance of genetic effects on development. It is also important to think very carefully about how genes affect development; I say "think" at this stage because we are only at the beginning of understanding how it may be that little chunks of DNA give rise to the complexities of form and function of a living organism (see, e.g. Bouchard, 1993, 1994; Greenough, 1986, 1991; Jensen & Sinha, 1993; Johnson, 1993; Rose, 1995; Thompson, 1993; Vernon, 1993). Again, it is here that there are really interesting questions. What are the "proximal processes" (Bronfenbrenner & Ceci, 1994) that lie between the genotype and the phenotype? Many such processes will be best described at a physiological level; psychologically, they are likely to be interactions between the developing person and the persons, objects and symbols in their environments which continue over time and involve a two-way flow between the internal and the external, and which are subject to cultural variation and historical change. They will vary as a joint function of the individual's genotype, phenotype and history, both immediate and more remote events, and the nature of the developmental outcomes being considered.

Given the possible range of gene–environment interactions and the lack of information to date about how DNA is linked to eventual behaviour, there is much uncertainty about how genes influence development. Molecular genetics is progressing rapidly (see, e.g. Rose, 1995) and both developmental behaviour geneticists and mainstream psychologists will need to take careful account of its findings. The model we need to develop here is not yet clear, but some introductory points can be made. The development of cognition, like most human behavioural traits, will depend on a complex interplay of more than one gene and of more than one environmental influence, operating in a complex inter-reaction over an extensive period of time. This "multifactorial inheritance", as I have argued elsewhere (Meadows, 1993), will not bear a very close resemblance to Mendelian inheritance. His garden pea plants had genes for seed colour and smoothness that operated in the simple all-or-none fashion which he elegantly described, but there is never going to be a gene, or even a set of genes, which control cognition, or any part of cognition, in quite this way. Instead, there will be a delicate and intricate pattern of interaction between the effects of a large number of genes as they express themselves within environments over the whole long period of development. We still know almost nothing about what this will be like in normal development. Even in those cases where a genetic anomaly leads to catastrophic outcomes, as for example in phenylketonuria, we are only beginning to understand development. Some other genetic anomalies have effects on the structure of the brain and on cognitive development. Down's syndrome, for example, leads to a high incidence of neurological disorders, including smaller and lighter brains with abnormal convolutions in certain areas, a reduction in the total number and density of neurones, and abnormal patterns of dendrites connecting neurones. Most Down's individuals are severely mentally handicapped, though there are considerable individual differences. These are associated with differences in the children's experience of formal and family efforts to support their cognitive development (Carr, 1988). It may be that patterns of interaction between Down's children and adults may be distorted, with possible effects on their cognition.

FURTHER STUDIES OF ADOPTION AND COGNITIVE DEVELOPMENT

An important French adoption study (Schiff & Lewontin, 1986; Schiff, Duyme, Dumaret, & Tomkiewicz, 1982) traced a sample of 32 children adopted within the first month of life into upper-middle-class families. Their biological mothers and putative fathers were all unskilled workers. The children's IQ scores and school careers were compared with schoolchildren in the general population, belonging to their original and adoptive social classes, and also with their biological half-siblings. The children in this last group had the same biological mother as the adopted children, though most had a different biological father, and were near them in age. However, they had not been adopted into middle-class families; instead, they were being reared in unskilled workers' families, mostly with their biological mother, though some were with foster-parents or grandparents.

It is quite clear from the scores in Table 5.3 that the IQs and the school careers of the adopted children and their non-adopted half-sibs were different from each other, and strongly resembled their social class of rearing—a marked shared environmental effect. The social class contrasts were particularly marked in their school histories: upper-middle-class children were much more likely to make uninterrupted progress through school. This finding is similar to many studies of the association between social class and school achievement; in general, middle-class children are less likely to become educational failures or under-achievers. Mild mental retardation is strongly associated with low SES, low levels of maternal education and worse housing and health, and does not usually explain itself in terms of overt brain damage or genetic abnormality, while severe mental retardation usually has some demonstrable physical cause and is not class-linked to the

TABLE 5.3

**School careers and IQ scores of French children adopted into middle-class families:
Comparisons with social class of origin and general population**

Children's social class	Sample	School history			IQ			
		No. of failures among 32 children of age of adopted and sibling sample	Failure rate (%) (remedial class)	Serious failure rate (%) (permanent special education)	Group IQ test		WISC IQ	
					Average	% below IQ of 85	Average	% below IQ of 85
Unskilled workers	Half-siblings of adopted children	16.1	66	33	95.1	21	94.2	25
	National surveys	16.5	67	34	95.0	21	–	
Upper middle class	Adopted children	4	17	3	106.8	5	110.6	3
	National surveys	4	17	3	110.0	3	–	
National norms		11.2	46	18	99.2	16	100.0	16

Source: Meadows (1993, p.183; adapted from Schiff & Lewontin, 1986, p. 90).

same degree (Broman et al., 1987). The preschool intervention studies of the Head Start initiative and its successors similarly suggest that the expectations of educational success or difficulty which the child, the parents and the schools hold, will interact with objective performance to produce worse educational careers for disadvantaged children than for more advantaged ones.

A further French adoption study (Capron & Duyme, 1989) similarly found that the social class you were adopted into made a 12–15 point difference in your IQ score, and a similar effect on your school achievements, though the children of more intelligent parents tended to have better outcomes. The same is found with antisocial behaviour (Duyme, 1988, 1990). Similar results have been found in some British studies (Tizard, 1977).

INTERVENTION STUDIES

Anxieties about the persistence of low educational achievement among the lowest socio-economic strata of society have led to various social interventions intended to combat the effects of poverty and disadvantage. From the 1960s, Project Head Start was the umbrella for a number of American projects in which children from the sorts of backgrounds where achievement in the school system was commonly low were given a period of preschool experience, usually brief, intended to forestall later poor school performance. This "inoculation" model, where the early improved experience was supposed to prevent the child from later succumbing to disadvantage, would not now be regarded with as much enthusiasm as it was then. The immediate result of such interventions was typically a rise in IQ scores which then reduced as time passed, so that after a couple of years in most studies the intervention group did not have higher scores than the control group. The inoculation did not seem to prevent failure for the disadvantaged children, and a number of commentators concluded that "compensatory education has been tried and it has failed" (Jensen, 1969).

Such a pessimistic conclusion was premature. The Head Start initiative varied a great deal in the content of its programmes, the duration of the intervention, the characteristics of the target group, the adequacy of the controls, and the sophistication of the analyses of the outcomes. Studies carried out with research in mind (e.g. Lee, Stigler, & Schnur, 1988) found Head Start closing the gap between the achievement of the most disadvantaged children and that of the more advantaged. Large-scale analyses of the interventions which were suitable for research (Consortium for Longitudinal Studies, 1983; Lazar & Darlington, 1982; Woodhead, 1985, 1988; Zigler & Styfco, 1993; Zigler & Valentine, 1979) suggested that a properly conducted preschool intervention could lead to short-term gains in IQ which were followed by better school achievement and motivation, and eventually by less risk of school failure, unemployment and deviant anti-social behaviour. In the very influential High/Scope Project (which although nominally "Piagetian" centres on a "Plan, Do, Review" cycle, which looks rather Vygotskian), it has been calculated that the costs of the initial intervention were recovered many times over in the reduction it brought about in the need for special education, unemployment benefits, legal and prison expenditure, and so forth (Berrueta-Clermont, 1984). There seems to be little doubt that such interventions can make a significant difference to the intellectual progress of children from the most disadvantaged social groups, who would otherwise fail in the main-stream educational system. The maintenance of respectable reading and maths scores, and an avoidance of educational difficulties so great that the child has to repeat a grade, seem to follow from high- quality interventions in Head Start and in other, later projects (e.g. Huston, 1991; Reynolds, 1994; Sylva, 1994; Zigler & Muenchow, 1992). There are some signs that parental involvement in the intervention is an important part of its success, though typically there are no data on how the parents' interaction with children was affected by the intervention.

British data (Clark, 1988) also support the importance of high-quality early education. In a population cohort study, for example, Osborn and Milbank (1987) showed an effect at age 10 from having attended an educationally oriented preschool: those children who had not attended any preschool were behind those who had on measures of reading, language and maths, and tended to have more behaviour problems. This might suggest that preschool attendance has benefits even for children who are not severely disadvantaged. The quality of the preschool again seems to be important, with some signs that children develop expectations of how to use the material and social resources around them, which may then carry over into the infant reception class. Meadows and Cashdan (1988), for example, trained nursery school teachers into a more Vygotskian style of discussion with their pupils, and found consequent changes in the children's approach to their teachers and their dialogue with them. Jowett and Sylva (1986) found that the graduates of nursery classes that had been comparatively learning-oriented were more likely than the graduates of a more free-play-oriented playgroup to settle well into the academic demands of the reception class and to take a more autonomous and purposeful approach to their work and play. Howes (1988, 1990) and Melhuish (personal communication) find analogous results in studies of day-care. The quality of adult–child interaction seems to be an important predictor of the effects of day-care.

One of the most interesting intervention projects of the Head Start period was the Milwaukee Project (Garber, 1988; Garber & Hodge, 1989). This has been the subject of much controversy (see, e.g. Garber & Hodge, 1989; Jensen, 1989), partly because of a scandal which involved one of the project's directors though not the project itself, and partly because of disputes about the extent of, and the reasons for, the rise in IQ scores that was brought about in the intervention group. It deserves a fairly full account here, both because the intervention changed adult–child interaction and thus is directly relevant to this book, and for the light the controversy casts on the difficulties of assessing changes in intelligence and cognition.

The Milwaukee Project aimed at preventing mental retardation in the infants of low-IQ, impoverished black Milwaukee women. The mothers and children studied were from severely disadvantaged areas of Milwaukee with poor housing, low levels of income and education, high unemployment rates, and a high prevalence of mental retardation in the population. The mothers' IQs were 75 or below on the WAIS; earlier work had shown that the children of such mothers tended to score at a normal level on the earliest baby intelligence tests but to decline in score through infancy and childhood, reaching the same low level as their mothers by the beginning of the school years. These children were seen to be at risk of mild mental retardation, partly no doubt because of the genotypes they inherited from their parents and because of their social disadvantage, but also and most importantly because of the understimulating environment which they were assumed to receive from their mothers. Low SES was not their only risk factor, nor was an unpromising genotype; they were seen to be at risk primarily because their low-IQ mothers were not expected to be able to provide them with cognitively stimulating interaction:

> The experience which mothers are capable of providing is determined in large part by their own sophistication in cognitive style. By definition, retarded mothers lack sophistication in those mental processes which comprise abstract and conceptual reasoning. Although they may be loving and caring mothers, they may simply not be capable of effectively or adequately mediating the intellectual microenvironment for their children in order to promote what is considered a "normal" rate of mental development (Garber & Hodge, 1989, p. 268).

The researchers predicted that the intellectual level of these children would decline over infancy and childhood; the aim of the intervention was not to raise their IQs but to prevent them from declining. A sample of at-risk babies was identified and allocated alternately to an intervention or experimental group and a control group. The 17 babies in the experimental group were taken each day to a specially equipped house in the neighbourhood where they were looked after by "paraprofessional infant caregivers", who were not formally trained in child development or education but were "warm, caring and language facile individuals" who interacted with their charges in a warm and responsive way. The babies thus had what the project researchers describe as parenting comparable to what normally functioning parents provide for their children. Their mothers, meanwhile, attended an on-the-job training programme and received such advice and support as they needed with dealing with general social problems and childcare. No attempt was made to change their own interaction with their children, although they did have some opportunity to see how the paraprofessional caregivers interacted with the babies. As the children grew older, the adult–child interaction shifted from one-to-one towards more group activities, though still centring on things "which parents naturally engage in to teach their children" (Garber & Hodge, 1989, p. 271). Between 2 and 4 years of age there was an emphasis on shared activities in art, music, storytelling, and so forth, and between 4 and 6 years of age pre-reading and pre-maths components, taught by two certified preschool teachers, were added. Self-directed behaviour and responsibility for task completion were encouraged, and in general there was the "achievement press" associated with parenting of high achieving children.

The control group, meanwhile, and also a "low-risk contrast group" from the same area whose mothers' IQs were over 100, remained with their mothers and were only involved in periodic assessment of their DQs (Developmental Quotients) and IQs. The intervention continued until the beginning of statutory schooling.

Figure 5.1 shows that the intelligence test scores of the control group fell as expected over the period when they were living with low-intelligence, impoverished, perhaps understimulating parents. There was a steep decline through infancy, and perhaps some further fall thereafter. The low-risk contrast group showed fairly steady scores from 2 to 14 years of age, apart from a sudden increase between 42 and 48 months, and an even more sudden decrease between 48 and 54 months, which looks like a measurement error at 48 months. The experimental group's scores rise from 10 to 24 months and remain steady until 48 months; there is some decline between 48 and 72 months, but from 84

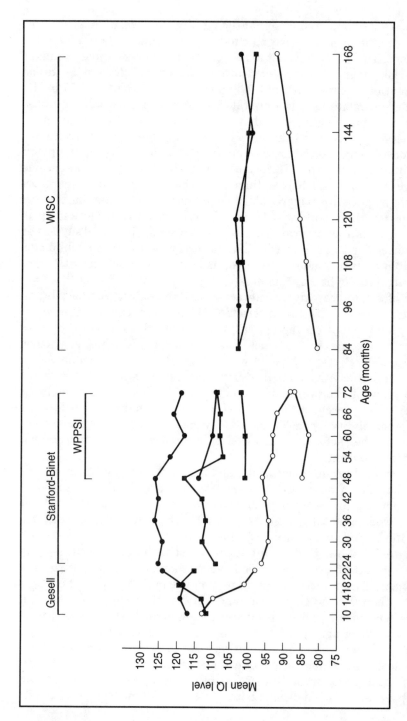

FIG 5.1. Profiles of mean DQ and IQ scores for the experimental (●), control (○) and low-risk contrast (■) children. Adapted from Garber and Hodge (1989).

months their scores are steady and very like those of the low-risk, no-intervention group. The early one-to-one part of the intervention seems to have a particularly marked effect on IQ scores. This looks as if it might be a demonstration that you can achieve normal IQ scores through stimulating interaction with an adult, either with your biological mother if her own intelligence level is normal and she provides you with a normal genotype for intelligence plus an adequate level of interaction, despite living in conditions of severe disadvantage; or by getting such interaction from an unrelated adult, although your own mother does not provide extra stimulation and perhaps did not provide you with a very satisfactory genotype for intelligence. If your mother's intelligence level is low, and you live in poverty, then your IQ score is likely to decline from a normal level to a low one, either because of a problematic genotype, the accumulating effects of poverty, a lack of stimulating interaction, or some combination of these.

While this is a possible interpretation, it has to be a tentative one. There are a number of problems with these data. First, the numbers are very small. This means that measurement errors can have a large effect, as in the case, perhaps, of the peak in scores for the low-risk contrast group at 48 months. Second, it was not always possible to ensure that the testers were blind to which group the children came from, so some scores may have been biased. This is always a problem in assessing interventions, where often the testers can guess the child's group membership correctly by the way the test is approached, even if it is not officially known to them. Third, the graph shows the difficulty of assessing a characteristic that changes over time. Different measures of "intelligence" are used for babies, for younger and older preschool children, and for older children. These produce different mean levels, as may be seen from the comparison of Stanford-Binet scores and WPPSI scores between 48 and 72 months, and between these and the WISC from 84 months on. As these discrepancies are known in other much larger samples, some adjustments can be made, but these mean that the status of the tests is that of an estimate rather than that of a measurement. Nevertheless, unless there is some principled reason why these problems should affect the groups differently, they obscure the size of the effect associated with the intervention rather than removing it altogether.

Garber (1988; Garber & Hodge, 1989) asserts that the intervention successfully halted the decline in IQ which could otherwise have been expected for the experimental group and which was seen to occur in the control group. Jensen (1989) believes that the apparent prevention of a decline was spurious, largely made up of specific training effects, because the curriculum of the intervention closely resembled the content of the intelligence tests used, and that there was no real effect on the children's underlying level of "g". Certainly, it is a problem in assessing an individual's "g", or innate general intelligence (what Eysenck, 1986, lists as "Intelligence A"), that so many intelligence tests (measuring "Intelligence C") include items that can be taught, and often are, being part of parents' informal curricula or schools' more formal ones. Short of using measures which are not at all affected by educational experience, there is no way round this problem (Meadows, 1993). However, as Garber and his colleagues were not attempting to raise "g" but to avert a decline in IQ scores, this is not a serious difficulty for the Milwaukee Project. Garber would presumably argue that "g" is less important in this context than what you can do with it.

What is a major problem for our present purposes is that we do not know much about the interaction between adults and children. It is conceivable, for example, that not having to cope with both their children and their poverty all day, every day, made the mothers of the intervention group much more able to provide stimulation for their child which may have contributed to the maintenance of normal IQ scores. Or, they may have retained more confidence in a child who came bouncing home from an interesting day at the Infant Stimulation Centre than in one who had been with them in hardship all day. It would be very interesting to know whether the parenting given by the paraprofessionals to the intervention group resembled that of the low-risk mothers in their disadvantaged homes or indeed ordinary middle-class mothers. Nor should we stop at an adult-to-child effect. It seems very likely that the more stimulated children learned to evoke different patterns of adult behaviour, so that the children could well have had an effect on their mothers, caregivers, testers and, later, teachers. Without much more documentation of this sort of level of detail, it is impossible to see how the intervention actually brought about its effect. Concentration on IQ scores as the principal measure of both entry level and outcome is understandable but inadequate for both the assessment and the explication of developmental change.

The educational achievement of the children in the Milwaukee Project was also assessed as they passed through the early stages of the normal school system. Before they entered school, the experimental group scored above the 50th percentile on the Metropolitan Readiness Battery, which assesses a range of reading-readiness and other school skills, while only three of the control group children scored over the 33rd percentile. Four years later, the experimental group still scored higher than the control group on mathematics and reading, though the difference was no longer any more than marginally significant. More of the control group children received special educational attention from their schools because they were experiencing difficulties in school; but many children in all three groups had reports of negative attitudes and behaviour or discipline problems in their school records. The normal level of intelligence shown by the intervention group and the low-risk controls was not sufficient to prevent educational failure. The Milwaukee Project prevented the expected decline in IQ scores over the period of intervention, but Garber and Hodge state that it had less effect on the motivation, energy, persistence, work habits, interests, values and opportunities that are also necessary for school achievement. Ideally, the project would have assessed these too, instead of focusing on IQ scores. Nevertheless, it seems clear that the intervention had not been able to do away with the school difficulties associated with poverty and disadvantage, despite being intensive and expensive. Improving the child's preschool experience of interaction with adults had prevented a decline in IQ, but that was not itself enough for continued good functioning. It is an uncomfortable but necessary reminder that we cannot expect a single inoculation against poverty to do much to protect against its effects.

The data on the effectiveness of preschool education show that it is normally beneficial for children to participate in good-quality playgroups, nursery education, or special intervention projects. They also suggest that "good-quality" could be unpacked into a central emphasis on Vygotskian adult–child interaction, which leads to children having a mastery orientation to their activities so that they involve themselves in school work with enthusiasm and confidence, and work for the intrinsic pleasure of meeting challenges, rather than opting out of intellectual effort or meeting any cognitive demands with a "I can't do it" attitude. Children whose later educational experience allows them to use this approach, and who are supported in their further efforts to appropriate the skills the culture requires, are set up for educational success and a positive sequence of cognitive development. But if the later stages of their education do not allow the children to use the skills of "learning how to learn", which they acquired by being scaffolded in their preschool years, the effects of preschool education may "wash out".

DAY-CARE

Studies which look at patterns of parent–child behaviour may find associations between parent "input" and child "outcome" that can be dismissed as due to the genes they both share, as being correlates at different points in the life cycle of the genetic continuity which is the major causal variable (Rowe, 1994). Such a dismissal overlooks the point that although the genes may indeed programme both the parents' behaviour and the child's, they may also need the parents' behaviour as a direct cause of the child's. Something analogous to this occurs in other species, for example in the development of birdsong (Macfarlane, 1987). Genes may be the ultimate cause, but interaction may be an equally necessary proximal one.

One way of sorting out the genetic and environmental issues to some degree is to examine settings where the child's caretaker is not also his or her parent. A recent study of day-care in Chicago (Clarke-Stewart, 1994) provides some very helpful data. They were concerned to fill the gaps in our knowledge of the relative effects of family and day-care experiences on young children, to explore children's experiences in a wide range of settings, to examine how these experiences were related to the children's development using a wide range of measures and to compare care by mother, other home-based care with related and unrelated people, and care in group settings. Altogether, 150 children who were 2–3 years of age at the outset were seen nine times over a period of about 14 months, during the morning and the afternoon in whatever setting or settings they normally spent the day, and at dinnertime and when going to bed, thus ensuring a good sampling of their day. Most of the sample were white and most of the families were professional or middle-class, with both the father and the mother having a college education. Single-parent families were excluded from the sample. The extremes of the social class distribution were not included. There was what seems a high level of claimed parent involvement with young children, less surprising perhaps given the voluntary nature of their involvement in the study; all the fathers claimed to spend some time in child care, half of them claiming to be actively involved with their children or responsible for them for at least 4 hours a day! A quarter of the mothers were working with, or had worked with, young children. This is a fairly well-off and rather child-centred sample, which makes the differences in interaction and outcome all the more interesting. These were families well within what Scarr (1992) calls the "expectable good environment"; though even here, contrary to Scarr's predictions, there do seem to be outcome differences.

It will be useful first to describe the general pattern of experiences of these children. The 2-hour dinnertime observation period often involved the child being alone for a significant part of the time, or playing with brothers or sisters, or watching television. About half played with their fathers and/or mothers, or were read to (most often by their mother). Older children got less attention from their parents, and there were no significant sex differences in behaviour except that fathers spent slightly more time teaching their sons than their daughters.

Socio-economic status and parents' behaviour were linked. High SES parents, both mothers and fathers, were less authoritarian, offering their children more choices and less discipline. The fathers read to their children more, and the children spent less time simply watching either their parents or TV during the dinnertime period. Mothers who were more knowledgeable about child development did not behave any differently towards their children than those who had less professional expertise, but the fathers in these families were less demanding and controlling of their children. Mothers who were more satisfied with their roles talked, taught and read to their children more, and had higher expectations of and more positive feelings for them; the fathers in these families were more affectionate towards their children and read to them more—a family pattern of active and enjoyable parenting. Children with working mothers interacted more with their fathers over dinnertime, though the quality of parental interaction overall was comparable in families with working and non-working mothers. Whatever "quality time" there was in these families, it didn't show up much at this time of the day; the children heard an average of 82 utterances from their fathers and 255 from their mothers—often demands for the child to do something, more rarely instructions or explanations, more rarely still helping or giving lessons (less than 3 minutes, on average).

The children's daytime experiences were more varied; indeed, variability was the data's main characteristic. For example, the number of utterances directed from the caregiver to an individual child ranged from almost none to nearly 900 in 2 hours; the amount of time a child spent playing alone with a toy ranged from none at all to more than an hour and a half, and the amount of time a child spent in "lessons" varied in the same way. Compared with home at dinnertime, there was much less expression of affection; most children were read to or sung to or given a "lesson" about something, but these tended to be brief. Daytime interaction with adults rarely involved sustained, positive and stimulating interaction, even if the child was in home day-care rather than a group setting. Mothers at home with their children during the day interacted with them more than they did at dinnertime, but the frequency of interaction of father and mother combined at dinnertime was greater than the mother alone during the day. These 2- and 3-year-olds were certainly not receiving long hours of intensive scaffolding from their caretakers in any settings.

Clarke-Stewart and her colleagues find ample evidence that children's cognitive development was affected by their experiences at home and in day-care. Children whose cognitive development was advanced received more stimulation, such as talking, teaching, reading and group education from their teachers. They spent less time watching

TV; they also interacted less with their peers, but spent more time playing with older children. Participation in these educational activities seemed to be even more important for 4-year-olds than for the younger children. The same pattern of differences between more and less advanced children was found at home in the evenings and in the day-care settings both morning and afternoon. Children whose cognitive development was proceeding faster had more frequent stimulating interactions with adults and older children; and development was most enhanced when the caregivers were less controlling and demanding, more responsive, offered the child choices, and read and sang to the child. When a caregiver was also the child's parent, this faster development may partly have been due to a favourable genetic inheritance which expressed itself as better teaching by the parent and better learning by the child. When a caregiver was not also the child's parent, the causal chain may have involved the child's experience of the adult's actions, though it could still have been the case that the child was evoking the adult's behaviour as well as responding to it. Both at home and in day-care, adult input at the first round of measurements was a good predictor of a child's cognition at the second round of measurements a year later, whereas the child's earlier cognition was not correlated at all with later input measurement. For example, even with year 1 cognition scores partialled out, the correlation coefficients between child cognition at year 2 and caregiver reading, teaching and responsiveness at year 1 were between 0.25 and 0.30, while the correlations between year 1 cognition and year 2 caregiver behaviour were approximately zero. This pattern of results, and the similarity of behaviour which seems to be effective across settings, argue I think for a direct effect of the caregiver's behaviour on the child. Even though all these children were in environments which could not be described as disadvantaged, the amount of "scaffolding" interaction between child and adults varied, and on the whole the cognitive outcomes were better for the child if there was more scaffolding rather than less.

Melhuish (personal communication), examining differences in the quality of interaction between caregivers and young children in different sorts of day-care, found variations within each setting that were associated with the child's cognitive progress, as measured by vocabulary, at ages three and six. Children who had been talked to more, and whose attempts to communicate had been responded to more, were more advanced at both ages. Again, this suggests that children's development is facilitated by child-contingent and warm interaction with adults who know the child well enough to be responsive and to scaffold.

TEACHERS AS FACILITATORS OF
COGNITIVE DEVELOPMENT

The focus of this book is on parents' interaction with their children as a factor in cognitive development. However, I think it of interest to examine briefly how children's interaction with unrelated adults who have a formal responsibility for their learning affects the children's cognitive development—similarities may help to bolster the case for parent–child interaction, whereas differences could lead us towards more specificity.

Children spend a great deal of their lives away from their parents in our society, even before they are of school age (see Clarke-Stewart, 1994, for recent data), but once they are in school that is the main setting in which their learning is supposed to take place.

It has to be said, of course, that the obvious differences between schools and homes, or between teachers and parents, regarding curriculum, staffing, funding, assessment, knowledge of the individual child and of children in general, and vested interests (Mayall, 1994), are so great that the viability of school-based scaffolding is problematic, to say the least. What is more, the eventual result of good scaffolding is that the learners become able to scaffold themselves, thus reducing the need for assistance from a more expert person. The child who has benefited from parent–child scaffolding at home may need teacher–child scaffolding less than children who have not been shown how to support endeavours to learn. Nevertheless, it could be that effective school teaching has significant elements of scaffolding.

There has been an enormous amount of research on why some schools or teachers seem to produce better cognitive achievement (or exam performance) than others (for reviews, see Brophy, 1986; Brophy & Good, 1986; Cole, 1990; Fraser, 1989; Mortimore et al., 1988, 1989; Rutter, 1985; Rutter, Maughan, Mortimore, & Ouston, 1979; Snow et al., 1991; Stevenson & Baker, 1987; Sylva, 1994; Tizard, Blatchford, Farquhar, & Plewis, 1988; Weinstein, 1991). I will focus here only on what can be gleaned from the research about whether effective schooling can be seen to involve the same sort of scaffolding as seems to be associated with effective cognitive functioning in the family.

It is not an easy matter to distinguish which characteristics of schools or teachers are associated with better performance by pupils. As well as disagreements about how to measure pupils' "better" performance and school and teacher characteristics, there is the directionality problem and the multiple influence problem. Teachers' behaviour may affect pupils' performance, but it is also affected by them; interaction with a bright and keen student may allow for far more precise analysis and incisive attack on a school task than interaction with a pupil who is less able or less willing. Furthermore, pupils are not only taught by their teachers; they are taught by their peers, their families, the outside world and most importantly perhaps by themselves. (For some pupils, the main role of the school should perhaps have been to keep out of the way. Charles Darwin, for example, had a very undistinguished school career, in part because the curriculum at the time centred on passive learning of Latin and Greek and this did little for his already developing talents in natural history.) Studies of school effectiveness have to take into account these issues; research is complicated by differences in the level of skills, knowledge and motivation that children start from, by differences in their abilities, by differences in their cognition-related activities outside school, by problems in measuring achievement, by problems in identifying and measuring relevant school or teacher characteristics, and so forth.

Among the school, teacher or classroom interaction characteristics that seem to be associated with better pupil performance are the following. Students learn best when they are engaged in academic tasks which are clearly introduced and which they can proceed through steadily, making consistent progress with few failures (ideally almost none when they have to work independently, and not many when the teacher is there to provide feedback and guidance); when the teacher has established a classroom orientation towards conscientious academic work, and supervises and instructs actively within the classroom; and when the teacher's behaviour supports the students' efforts through such behaviour as question sequences which establish easy facts which have to be combined to answer a harder problem, allowing an appropriate time for a student to produce an answer, providing regular and extensive feedback, praising specifically rather than generally, and acknowledging achievements in a positive but non-intrusive way. This looks very like scaffolding. If it is, it has to be differentiated to fit the characteristics of the learners. Very young pupils need more instruction in the routines and procedures of the classroom and of learning, and being involved in the development of basic skills they need frequent opportunities to practise them and receive feedback on them. Older pupils who have internalised how to be a pupil and are now applying well-learned skills may not need to participate in the scaffolding of the activity so overtly, and may learn with more impersonal instruction; they can provide a great deal of scaffolding for themselves. Similarly, low achievers need more structuring of their learning by their teachers: more active instruction, more feedback, higher success rates and smaller steps in cognitive demands, more practice, more support and more encouragement. Thus scaffolding in the classroom has to be adjusted to the individual's current competence and permanent or temporary idiosyncracies. No wonder that teaching is such a demanding and highly skilled activity!

A number of experimental teaching projects have used scaffolding ideas in approaches to more effective teaching of children who are not performing well in schools. The work of Ann Brown and her colleagues (Brown & Campione, 1986, 1988; Brown & Palincsar, 1989; Brown, Palincsar, & Armbruster, 1984) is particularly interesting. Their teaching activities are composites, involving context setting, modelling, examples, practice, explanation and transfer. Explicit and well-structured instruction can teach children to execute many cognitive strategies; generalising this learning to new tasks requires learning about how, when and where the strategies can be used. The teaching adult has many tasks: to direct attention to currently relevant features of what is being done; to suggest what else might be considered, remembered or done; to model appropriate actions or strategies; to supervise and provide feedback on the child's actions; gradually to shift responsibility to the child without incurring a risk of failure. Such procedures appear to have given good results in Brown's studies, and in similar ones by other workers (e.g. Tharp & Gallimore, 1988); they are applicable from preschool (e.g. Blank, 1973; Blank, Rose, & Berlin, 1978; Meadows & Cashdan, 1988) to secondary school and beyond. Pupils who are poor, unconfident learners may benefit from them particularly, perhaps because pupils who are already good learners can scaffold themselves except in very novel areas. Furthermore, it does seem that this way of learning has good motivational effects, and makes appropriate transfer of learning more likely.

"Transfer" of learning has been argued to be one of the most important components of cognitive development (e.g. Brown et al., 1983; Goswami, 1992). Although it is not a simple concept (see, e.g. Meadows, 1993), successful transfer seems to involve grasping the important structural features of a task, comparing these with analogous tasks, and taking the risk of "going beyond the information given" and applying the old skills to the new situation where they may possibly be useful. This is more likely to happen if the learning of the first task has included appreciating what sort of task it is and what range of application the skills or information which have been taught might have, and clarifying as far as possible why they were effective. This sort of discussion is a common part of scaffolding and the appropriation of cultural tools. It is at least arguable that learning in a scaffolding situation facilitates transfer, avoiding the acquisition of "inert knowledge"; it is also possible that progress through the zone of proximal development often includes the development of transfer to increasingly distant situations.

This discussion of school learning and teaching has been too brief to do the subject justice. However, it supports the importance of scaffolding as a means to producing effective cognitive development, and somewhat strengthens the case for interaction between parent and child, rather than genetic resemblance in itself, being a cause of the fine-tuning of the child's cognitive development. The next chapter looks at parent–child pairs where there are anomalies in the interaction, to examine whether these are associated with anomalous cognitive development.

CHAPTER SIX

Parents and children
with scaffolding problems

INTRODUCTION

The research I have discussed so far suggests that there is an association between parent–child interaction and the child's cognitive development, such that within the normal range of child ability and parent–child interaction, those children who receive more scaffolding from their parents may do better cognitively and educationally than those who receive less. In the last chapter, I reviewed the complexity of the causes of this association. First, it is complicated by real social address differences in other conditions (such as health and educational experience), which also affect cognitive development (see also Hiester et al., 1994). Second, and even more importantly, there is no simple one-way effect of parent input on child outcome, but rather the interacting parent and child react to each other's characteristics and the history of their relationship, in ways which are affected by their genes, by their prior learning and by their expectations of the future, in a very complicated interdependence of genes and environments. While there is no significant disagreement that both genes and environments are relevant to cognitive development, neither is well understood, and there is debate about the causal mechanisms and their relative importance. If we look at parents and children in a comparatively narrow range of environments, as in the developmental behaviour genetics studies, then environmental and interaction effects will be hard to find. In this chapter, therefore, I want to look at some instances of parent–child interaction which are, for one reason or another, problematic. The hypothesis to be examined here is that if normal scaffolding interaction is a facilitator of cognitive development, children who do not get it will show significant cognitive deficits. In many cases, it makes little sense to locate the cause of difficulties in interaction between two people in one person rather than the other, but the organisation of the clinical literature does this as a first step, and the rest of this chapter uses this framework. I am going to look first at a number of cases where the parent's problems make it hard to support the child's cognitive development, then at some children whom it is peculiarly hard to scaffold. If parent–child interaction has any effect on children's cognitive development, then persistent individual differences in such interaction might lead to differences in the long-term outcome for the child. This need not be the case if the importance of adult–child interaction is simply that the child should experience some minimum quantity of it to trigger an autonomously generated development. But if more than that is required of the interaction, the pattern of individual differences in adult–child input and of differences in child output may tell us a great deal about how adult–child interaction is effective.

I must repeat the caution already given about supposing the only or major causal path runs from the parent to the child. There are real difficulties in determining who to attribute interaction to; we tend to think of parents (or teachers) doing things to affect children but to neglect (until we are actually parents or teachers ourselves) the ways in which children affect adults' behaviour. A two-way influence, indeed a long-lasting transaction, seems a more plausible developmental influence. In fact, much of the evidence on the early stages of language development and on scaffolding suggests that the adult's use of child-contingent responses is the crucial feature for speedy and effective development; rapid developers tend to have parents who pick up the child's own remarks, talk about the child's activities, establish a joint shared focus of attention, increase demands when the child has just succeeded, provide more support when the child has difficulties, and so on. As in the areas of attachment and socialisation, "responsiveness" (though not unproblematic in definition and measurement) seems to be an important facilitator of good development.

If this is so, then parents who are handicapped in providing child-contingent parenting are of particular interest. Their children will lack the experience that is being proposed as so peculiarly facilitating as to be necessary for good development, and therefore their development should show differences (and differences in the direction of less good functioning) compared with children who have had more child-contingent parenting. I will discuss some of the research on such groups now.

DEPRESSED MOTHERS AND CHILDREN'S COGNITIVE DEVELOPMENT

A substantial proportion of mothers of small children in Britain and the United States suffer from depression. In comparison with both men and childless women, women with children are at far higher risk of depression, and British population studies (e.g. Brown & Harris, 1978; Richman, Stevenson, & Graham, 1982) have found that 20–40% of women with children are depressed enough to be truly suffering from it, though not all of them will have sought medical help. A number of psycho-social variables are associated with an increased risk of depression: low socio-economic status, lack of a confiding relationship with husband, partner or close friend, marital discord, several preschool children (especially if they include twins) and no satisfying job.

"Depression" is a complex phenomenon, varying from case to case in severity and duration. It is basically a recurrent disorder with episodes of great distress and varying degrees of residual difficulty during the intervening periods. Most acute episodes resolve in 6–9 months, but a substantial proportion last for years. Depression is associated with anxiety and "personality disorders" such as aggression and undue dependence, and also with difficulties in life such as economic adversity, poor interpersonal relationships, bereavement, lack of social support, housing problems and marital conflict, instability, and break-up. It may also be associated with factors that are entirely or largely "in" the child, such as prematurity, multiple birth, serious handicap, "difficult" temperament. Mild depression may not be easy to diagnose in parents of young children, as it resembles the results of the sleep deprivation, anxiety and other stresses associated with the demands of parenting.

Whatever its causes, depression does have consequences which are highly relevant to the provision of child-contingent parenting. As Downey and Coyne (1990, p. 61) point out, child-contingent parenting of young children is a very demanding task:

> Parenting is a particularly complex form of social interaction. The sustained effortful behaviour that it involves is likely to prove difficult for depressed parents, especially when their children are young and exaggerated affective tone and a high tolerance for aversive behaviour is required.

A number of studies in Britain and North America have described the parenting difficulties of depressed mothers (see Coyne & Downey, 1991; Cummings & Davies, 1994; Downey & Coyne, 1990; Meadows, 1993; Rutter, 1990; Zahn-Waxler, 1995). Depressed mothers may become very withdrawn and despairing, which will make responsive and positive interactions with the child much less likely. Alternatively, they may become highly irritable, intrusive and controlling, showing a great deal of anger and hostility to the child. Neither withdrawn or hostile mothers are likely to manage to provide a normal amount or pattern of scaffolding, or other positive parenting. There will be less overt positive enjoyment of interaction with the child, less joint play and less imaginative cooperation: fewer of the child's overtures are responded to, little is done to facilitate social interaction, interaction is not managed in ways which allow conflicts to be anticipated and avoided, and the more frequent conflicts that therefore arise are allowed to result in hostile and escalating control and anger or in the mother caving in to the child's demands and abdicating her authority. Neither pattern of reaction maintains much child-contingent and positive interaction: the children will lack scaffolding, language which provides support and models for their own language and cognition, recognition of their personal achievements, opportunities to negotiate and discuss happenings, explanations and rationales as to why something is so or must be so, shared attention and joint play, mother's suggestion of links between the child's own activity now and their past experience, their future possibilities and the way the world is, and all the fun and positive feeling that goes with these. The mother becomes more likely to report that the child has behaviour problems; and there may be a shift from mother taking care of the child towards the child feeling a caretaking responsibility towards the distressed mother.

While deficits of these sorts have been seen in several studies of toddlers and their mothers, including children with non-organic failure to thrive (Puckering et al., 1995), there is much less on the later difficulties that they might bring about. The SLUFP studies (Cox, Puckering, Pound, & Mills, 1987; Meadows, 1993; Meadows & Mills, 1987; Mills & Funnell, 1983; Mills, Puckering, Pound, & Cox, 1985; Pound, Mills, Puckering, & Cox, 1982) do begin to provide the necessary longitudinal data.

The first stage of this study involved detailed observations of depressed and "control" mothers (the latter demographically similar to the former but without psychiatric symptoms) at home with their 2-year-old children, focusing on their joint activity and on episodes of control or distress. The children were observed again in any preschool setting they attended, and during their second term in the infant school (at age 6) when teacher ratings and scores on a computer vigilance task were added to the intelligence tests taken at 2 and 6 years of age. The mothers were interviewed extensively about their lives, marriages and circumstances when the children were 2 years old. They were all white, working-class, British-born, two-parent, inner-London families, with the father in employment at the start of the study.

There was variation in the parenting of the 2-year-olds within both the depressed group of mothers and the control group. Some of the depressed mothers were parenting with a great deal of sense and sensitivity, and their children were largely problem-free at both ages and in all settings. But the larger part of the depressed mothers reported that their children had extensive behaviour problems, and here the mother–child interaction showed a less promising pattern, especially if there was marital discord (see also Davies & Cummings, 1994) in the family. These mothers were less likely to respond to the overtures of their 2-year-olds, to extend their children's behaviour in "scaffolding" ways, to facilitate social interaction, and to pre-empt conflicts by managing the interaction and the environment so that problems did not reach a flashpoint and develop into overt conflict. They were more likely to be very withdrawn and despairing, or to be intrusive, critical and hostile, reacting to the child's distress with control and anger. There was less visible positive enjoyment of mother–child interaction, less joint involvement in activities, less creation of "links" relating the child's present activities to other relevant occasions, and less cooperation in imaginative play. In their interaction, there was less mother response to what the child said and did, less support for the child so that he or she could persist and solve a problem, less offering of useful representations of the world for the child to take on and re-represent, less demonstration of useful skills, and less metacognitive discussion of what was being done. Although there was no decrease in physical warmth and cuddles, some of this was not contingent on the child's desires, and seemed to be the mother using the child as a comfort object.

In our follow-up of these children, those who had had depressed mothers and behaviour problems at 2 years of age were in a comparatively poor state in their first year of school 3–4 years later. They were conspicuously less good at concentrating on school tasks and at developing their activity beyond a very simple repetitive level; their teachers rated them as significantly poorer on social and academic functioning, with many more problems being reported; they had much more difficulty with formal tests of intelligence and attention. Their verbal IQs were lower and their concentration spans (as measured by the WPPSI digit span tests) were reduced. In many ways, they were having great difficulty in engaging with the academic and social curriculum of the reception class; they spent long periods in inaction or fragmented activity, and might not even get involved in cooperative play with other children in the playground. Both their performance and their engagement with activities and tasks were impaired relative to the children who had earlier received better scaffolding. On the whole, they were underperforming and anxious children, passive and not a nuisance, but also not making much contribution to the class. Rather than acting-out aggressively, they were not engaging with the opportunities that school offered, and their level of achievement and enjoyment were low. They looked, in short, like depressed under-achievers, for whom school was an unwelcome challenge or even a source of distress. There was continuity between the level of problems at age 2 and the level of problems at age 6, and given the limited resources that the schools had to help such children to develop whatever talents they had, continuity of lack of involvement, lack of achievement and lack of enjoyment might be expected to continue.

The characteristics of these SLUFP children as they started school have also been observed in some North American samples of older children. Attention problems were found by a number of researchers (Cogill et al., 1986; Cohler et al., 1977; Jacobvitz & Sroufe, 1987; Wahler & Dumas, 1989), as well as negative self-concept and attributional style (Goldsmith & Rogoff, 1995; Hammen et al., 1987; Hammen, Burge, & Stansburg, 1990; Nolen-Hoeksma, Wolfson, Mumme, & Goskin, 1995) and guilt and anxiety (Radke-Yarrow, 1991; Teti, Gelfand, Messinger, & Isabella, 1995; Zahn-Waxler & Kochanska, 1990). As in other studies, depression in parents seemed to be associated with depression in children, perhaps as a modelled and learned coping style, perhaps because of a genetic predisposition to learned helplessness. What the SLUFP data additionally suggest is considerable continuity over an important period of learning to be a cognitive person, mediated by a deficit in parent–child interaction. There were some signs that if the parent's depression lifted, the child's behaviour subsequently improved. Longer maternal depression meant worse performance by the child.

There may perhaps be links between the absence of child-contingent scaffolding and problems in the child's attention and cognitive development via a purely cognitive route, for example less effective transfer of information from the mother to the child because she is attending less closely and empathetically to the child and picks up his or her cues of understanding or puzzlement less well. There may also be effects through the sadder and more negative emotional tone (Bettes, 1988; Breznitz & Sherman, 1987) of the mother–child interaction on both the child's cognition and the child's personality and emotional development—more occasions when what is communicated is helplessness in the face of a challenge, or the uselessness of effort (Goldsmith & Rogoff, 1995; Nolen-Hoeksma et al., 1995). (It is of course one of the problems of researching the association between any form of teaching and the consequent learning that what is actually learned may not be the overt curriculum content, but some ancillary message about the teacher or the learner or the subject matter, quite different from that which is officially intended to be taught.) Parenting which lacks responsiveness to the child, is non-contingent and non-facilitating, and does not extend the child's activity imaginatively, may be associated with slower and more limited development of cognition and language, with a depressed verbal IQ, with less symbolic play, and with impaired concentration and engagement in school. Parenting which deals with control issues by imposing obedience unilaterally or by totally abdicating control in the face of even minimal child resistance misses the opportunities for teaching a child to reason, negotiate, empathise and understand other persons that more responsive mothers might provide when they manage control issues more constructively, and the consequences at school age might include difficulties with classroom routine and cooperation with other children, as well as perhaps less empathy and understanding (cf. Dunn, 1988). Parenting which is sad and helpless seems to be associated with the development of child behaviour that is anxious, guilt-ridden and helpless, characteristics that will be of no help to a child who needs to be an enthusiastic "self-running problem-solver" able to acquire a full toolbag of cognitive skills and strategies so as to function well in any formal educational system, or even merely on IQ tests.

COGNITIVE DEVELOPMENT IN ABUSED CHILDREN

Children whose parents abuse them may be another group who are likely to miss out on sensitive scaffolding of their cognitive development. Again, this is far from being a homogeneous group, and even less is known about the cognitive progress of abused children than of the children of depressed mothers. (I believe, however, that the clinical impression is that such children often have impaired performance on cognitive tasks.) However, it does seem that abusive mothers have negative emotions about their abused children, and unrealistic expectations about their behaviour (Dix, 1991; Knutson, 1995). Their discipline techniques may be harsh and erratic, and their interaction with their children disorganised, unresponsive, and lacking in scaffolding and positive emotion. Dix (1991) suggests that these mothers may have problems with several behaviours relevant to scaffolding: with selection of goals, plans and expectations, with appraisals of ongoing success and failure, and with self-efficacy and self-control. Unlike the parents of socially competent children, who tend to be responsive, to express warmth and affection, to reason and communicate openly, to make appropriate demands for mature behaviour, to establish and enforce consistent rules, and to avoid arbitrary, restrictive and coercive control (e.g. Maccoby & Martin, 1983), they may not organise the child's experience in these ways and so not provide the same range of experience to draw positive lessons from. Their parenting may not be as successful in teaching children cooperative, responsive behaviour, social problem-solving skills, or positive knowledge of social relationships. Abusive parents have difficulty in monitoring their child's behaviour closely, and so could not scaffold it appropriately, or pre-empt potential disputes (as was important in the SLUFP study), or coordinate their own actions and concerns with those of the child. They may have real difficulties in eliciting positive behaviour from the child, who has learned to react coercively to the parent's negativity and coercion. They may have difficulty in establishing and communicating clear and realistic expectations of what should be done, either by themselves or by the child. Their emotional communications may be distorted, overly negative or ambiguous, and so a poor source of information on the parent's concerns or the parent's next action. From quite early in infancy, children use their parents' emotional reactions as a signal as to whether they should or should not continue the activity they have embarked on (e.g. Cicchetti, 1994). Children of abusive mothers often do not know what behaviour their mothers expect, do not think their mothers are acting cooperatively to promote their concerns, and do not value interactional strategies that are cooperative and responsive. They might not react appropriately to parental scaffolding even if it were provided for them.

The research questions in the literature on abused children do not on the whole derive directly from the "scaffolding" metaphor. The literature's theoretical focus is more on attachment, personality and socialisation than on cognition. However, it does contain a few hints of evidence that abusive parenting might lack scaffolding and responsivity and that these deficits might hamper the child's cognitive development. Cicchetti (1994), for example, describes work on young children's use of words that refer to internal mental states. Mastery of verbal labels for internal states (such as perceiving, wanting, wishing, being able and knowing) is an important component of communicating them, and also a possible route for sorting out some of the misunderstandings and misinterpretations that occur during interactions with other people. Mental state concepts can also be a useful part of the scaffolding process and of understanding other people. Maltreated toddlers, at the age when the use of such words is normally burgeoning, use fewer of them than normally parented children do, and in a more context-bound way, both when talking about themselves and when talking about other people. They are especially unlikely to speak about negative emotions, perhaps because these are too dangerous and painful in these families. Smetana and Kelly (1989) also found differences in social cognition between children who were and were not maltreated. Dunn (1988, 1993) showed that among a normally parented sample of preschool children, talking more about emotions and the problems of resolving disagreements leads to more sophisticated social cognition a couple of years later. Thus, the abused children were both immature in their use of internal state words and their judgements of antisocial acts, and missing out on discussions that seem to accelerate the development of social cognition.

Aber and colleagues (Aber, 1994; Aber, Allen, Carlson, & Cichetti, 1989) reviewed the literature on the effects of maltreatment on the development of young children. They suggest that the child's belief in his or her ability to deal competently with the environment and achieve mastery of it is damaged by abuse and insecure attachment. They also cite work which shows poorer performance on measures of cognitive maturity. These earlier findings are further supported by their own studies, which show maltreated children to be low on secure readiness to learn from novel adults. This index of cognitive maturity was also positively associated with parents' encouragement of the child's autonomy, with their enjoyment of the child, and with their access to community resources. Erickson, Egeland and Pianta (1989) found abused children functioning more poorly on cognitive tasks, failing to organise their behaviour effectively, or to persist in the face of difficulties when persistence would have solved the problem. They were easily distracted, unenthusiastic, non-compliant and impulsive, and also highly dependent on their teachers for help and support. Again, this looks like a history of inadequate or non-existent scaffolding leading to a failure to learn to scaffold oneself, and consequently to inadequate performance in the mainstream classroom. The timing of the period of maltreatment may have been particularly important in this sample. The children who were maltreated early in the preschool years were not functioning as well cognitively as the children whose abuse had begun at a later age, obtaining lower scores on the WPPSI and teacher ratings that were lower on confidence, assertiveness and creativity, even if they were no longer being maltreated. This may be a sign of a critical period for scaffolding during the first couple of years, with irreversible or only slowly reducing damage being done by maltreatment during that period, or it may be that although the degree of maltreatment had reduced so that it was no longer considered a danger to the child officially, the level of parenting after maltreatment had still been suboptimal. While we have no evidence that allows us to decide between these possibilities, in a recent study of "failure-to-thrive" children (Puckering et al., 1995), the researchers judged that the children's brain development might have been impaired by their early under-nutrition, and something of this sort might apply in the case of child abuse.

Erickson et al. (1989) describe their samples of maltreated children as anxious (inattentive, preoccupied, fidgety, having difficulty comprehending directions), having an abiding anger, unpopular, and having difficulty in meeting even the minimal demands of kindergarten. These are qualities that will evoke more negative behaviour from other people than confidence, competence and resilience would do. They are also qualities that will make positive engagement with cognitive challenges less likely. As with the children who had suffered a lack of scaffolding by their depressed mothers, the outcome to be expected within the mainstream education system is not good.

EXTREME DEPRIVATION: CHILDREN WHO RECEIVE VERY LITTLE ADULT–CHILD INTERACTION

Clinical studies of children living in the very unstimulating and unsupportive conditions provided by orphanages that focus on the physical health of children but neglect to allow them opportunities for relationships with the caregiving adults, have shown that the children tend to be behind normally reared children in their socio-emotional development, and in their cognitive skills (Goldfarb, 1945; Spitz, 1946). A more recent study of children in Romanian orphanages (Kaler & Freeman, 1994) found similar deficits on standardised cognitive and behavioural scales, on early social communication with adults, and on task orientation. The degree of deficit was not related to the child's birthweight or APGAR score, which suggests that the deficits were not caused by any gross organic disability. Lack of opportunity to engage with stimulating adults and interesting materials seems the more likely cause.

Skuse (1984, 1993) discusses the development of children who have been rescued from extreme abuse, neglect and deprivation. Most of the children he describes, and others, such as a Japanese pair described by Fujinaga, Kasuga, Uchida and Saiga (1990), were horribly neglected, deprived of all positive social stimulation, frequently beaten and physically confined. Experience of responsive, warm, culturally supportive interaction must have been at rock-bottom. All these children showed serious deficits in cognition, language, attention and social behaviour when first rescued from their abuse. For most of them, rehabilitation by being fostered in a good supportive and stimulating family group led to fairly rapid acquisition of language and cognitive skills, though socio-emotional well-being was slower to develop. Even these desperately deprived children seem to have functioned eventually within the normal range, though as most of their caregivers very properly gave rehabilitation a higher priority than research, the assessments made of their abilities were sometimes impressions rather than based on standardised tests. The deficits that they showed when first rescued argue that at least a minimum of adult–child interaction is necessary for cognitive development; their recovery argues that cognitive skills can develop later than normal, if good stimulation and support are provided. It is worth noting that these children were not expected to cope with normal schooling until they had already shown a great deal of recovery in more protective social settings. Some did eventually attend school, and even perform quite well there, but only after an initial period of therapy. Some never did well enough to enter into formal education or employment.

CHILDREN WHOM IT IS HARD TO SCAFFOLD

I have been trying to make a case that if parents do not provide their children with the warm, responsive, child-contingent interaction that neo-Vygotskian theory focuses on as a source of good cognitive development for the child, or with the culturally available functional equivalent, there may be persistent deficits in cognition, both at the pervasive level of difficulties in motivation and controlled selective attention, and in specific areas of language and cognition. Evidence from normal parents and children and from children of parents with difficulties in scaffolding has been presented. Some evidence from studies of children who are in some way difficult to scaffold now follows. It should be noted that I am not locating the source of the difficulty in the child, and in particular that there should be no implications of blame to any participant.

A recent review (Campbell, 1995) complements the work on problematic parenting which I have already discussed by looking at the interaction between mother and child where the child is seen as having behaviour problems. Consistently, for both preschoolers and school-age children, interaction with mother is more conflict-ridden and negative. Mothers of children who are hyperactive, aggressive or non-compliant are more impatient and power-assertive when interacting with them, more likely to ignore prosocial behaviour when it does occur and to reward negative behaviour with attention. Mothers of highly active children are less responsive to their children's needs and less clear in conveying their expectations about how something should be done, more negative and controlling during unstructured play and cleaning-up, and less likely to reward independent play. Mothers are less likely to follow through their own directives, thus allowing the child to get away with things more, and less likely to follow through a response to the child's provocations and requests. Children whose parents and preschool teachers agree that they are defiant, aggressive and hard to manage are engaged with more confrontations at home with their mothers, comply less with their mothers' requests and are less skilled in amusing themselves, spending more time in aimless activity and watching television, and less time in constructive solitary play. There is a shortage here of pleasurable joint play activities and conversations between mother and child, little positive mutual engagement, less turn-taking, less working together towards a shared goal. Whatever the original cause of these behaviours, they are associated with problems and deficits in interaction that surely contribute to the high degree of continuity that problems such as poor concentration, lack of compliance, over-activity and disruption typically show from preschool age to the school years, where they are associated with lower reading abilities and lower general intelligence, at least for boys. The hard-to-scaffold child's lack of scaffolding in the case of behaviour problems would seem to lead to deficits in cognition, engagement, persistence and achievement—and also, other studies suggest, lack of self-esteem.

Down's syndrome is the most common genetic anomaly leading to mental retardation. Most individuals with Down's syndrome are mentally handicapped, the majority being severely handicapped. There is a progressive decline in IQ scores from near normal in the early months of infancy to lower scores in the school years, with the Down's child having particular difficulty in making progress from sensori-motor intelligence to verbal and conceptual intelligence. There are particular problems in auditory processing, auditory memory and metacognition. Language comprehension may be better than language production. The overall pattern of development proceeds through the same sequence as in cognitively normal children, but there is less coherence between development in different domains and overall achievement falls farther and farther behind the normal level. Morss (1985) sees this pattern of developmental delay as reflecting poor learning style; Down's children seem to need more exposures to material before they learn spontaneously, and to lack cognitive strategies of transfer.

There is no doubt that the chromosomal anomaly which is the basis of Down's syndrome is the crucial cause of these cognitive effects. While we cannot identify a direct route from chromosome to cognitive behaviour, it is known that Down's individuals have a high incidence of neurological disorders, for example smaller and lighter brains with abnormal convolutions in some areas, a reduction in the total number and density of neurones, and abnormal patterns of dendrites connecting neurones. The central nervous system of Down's individuals who survive into mid-adulthood commonly develops the pathological changes characteristic of Alzheimer's disease. Furthermore, the genetic anomaly also gives rise to hearing difficulties and articulation problems, which contribute directly to language production and comprehension problems (Rondal, 1993). However, there are grounds for thinking that the sensory and central nervous system defects interact with environmental factors during development, and that some aspects of this interaction themselves give rise to handicap.

Down's individuals vary as much as genetically normal individuals do in their cognitive and personality characteristics. Some are profoundly handicapped, some can learn to read and to cope with normal schooling. A thorough longitudinal study by Carr (1988) helps to show the sources of these differences. Girls do better than boys on both IQ and educational tests; home-reared children do better than those reared away from home on verbal ability, reading-level and arithmetic tests, but not on IQ tests; non-manual SES children do better on language and arithmetic tests, reading accuracy and reading-level, despite not doing better on IQ tests. This seems largely to be the result of heroic efforts on the part of the parents to support their children's cognitive development.

These efforts perhaps deserve all the more praise when we remember that a number of studies have shown that there are commonly distortions in the interaction of Down's children and their parents that may make child-contingent scaffolding more difficult. Their hearing difficulties may be the cause of their low levels of verbal imitation compared with normal children (Chapman, 1995). During their first year, they show impairments in vocalisation, referential looking and intersubjective communication, which makes it harder for the parents to pick up on the child's own activity. There is reduced eye contact, less synchronicity of action, and less alternation of conversational turns. Mothers tend to become more directive and restricted, and while they remain highly responsive to the child's behaviour, as the child interacts less spontaneously the mother is more often the original initiator of the child action that she then responds to (Chapman, 1995; Gunn, 1985; Jones, 1979; Snow, 1995). Researchers working with Down's children (and other atypical developers) often find that they, too, are adopting ways of interacting with the children that are more directive and less contingent. It is possible that the more directive interaction is faciliatory for these children, and Lieven (1994) suggests it could be developmentally appropriate and so functionally equivalent. However it is different, and from the point of view of scaffolding theory, it might be expected to have different effects. Whether this is seen as an adult-to-child effect, or as the child evoking less helpful behaviour from the adult, hardly matters; what is important is to recognise that the child who needs facilitative interaction with other people more than most children do may actually be getting less of it. This is depressingly similar to the school experience of poor readers (Meadows, 1993), who are trained on the basic components of reading but tend to miss out on the higher level rewards it can bring.

The development of cognition and language in blind children has been of interest to philosophers and researchers for as long as there has been a theoretical emphasis on the role of experience in development. So far as interaction between blind children and adults is concerned, the research picture (Mills, 1993) of the blind child's cognitive development is of a number of problems that may be associated with differences in the child's experience of interaction with others; for example, difficulties in early preverbal communication because of the child's inability to monitor what the adult is looking at, and the adult's inability to use the direction the child is facing as a sign of what the child is attending to; later deficits in concept formation associated with difficulties in sorting and naming objects which cannot be seen; and late mastery of locational terms such as "on", "in" and "under". Adults' input language seems to include more imperatives, fewer descriptions and more bald labels, and more topics initiated by the adult rather than by the child. It would seem that the child's visual impairment leads to difficulties for adults in supporting their cognition, and that these may further hinder their cognitive development.

Children who are deaf before they begin to acquire language seem to suffer similar distortions in interaction with adults (Gallaway & Woll, 1994; Mogford 1993). Between 5 and 10% of deaf children are born to deaf parents, and if the parents use sign language the children will be able to acquire it as their first language. Deaf children of hearing parents, however, are much less likely to see fluent signing from infancy; their parents may only use spoken language, which the child cannot hear properly, or they may be learning a sign language or a supplementary system of signs to support the spoken language they address to their deaf child. These children find themselves in a situation in which they must learn language that is significantly different from the situation of a hearing child of hearing parents, and perhaps significantly more difficult.

There are fairly well-documented differences between the language of hearing mothers to deaf children and the child-directed speech which ordinary hearing children receive. Typically, both the quantity and the cognitive complexity of the mother's input is reduced. The flow of dialogue is limited because the child most often does not respond. Mothers have difficulty in attaining and retaining joint attention and reference in situations such as looking at a picture book. Interactions involve more control by the mother and in various ways, including the mother initiating more utterances and using more repetitions and imperatives. The earlier interpretation of this difference was that these mothers were inadvertently providing a less facilitating environment for their children's language development. However, Gallaway and Woll argue that "different" does not necessarily mean "worse". Mothers' utterances are in fact fairly well tuned to the level of their child's receptive language; the children who are receiving a lot of repetitions and directions may be at a point in their language development where such input is appropriate. They may be taking a different route to language use, rather than failing altogether.

When the child gets to school, teachers, too, may tend to be highly controlling, and children's initiatives may be discouraged or neglected, perhaps because the child's behaviour is more often hard to understand. Deaf pupils more rarely elaborate in response to repeated questioning (Wood et al., 1982), and rarely ask questions for clarification. Here, too, because the child's handicap makes scaffolding additionally difficult, children who may need scaffolding more than usual may be missing out on it, though it is crucial to recognise that spoken verbal interaction is not necessarily an essential part of scaffolding. There may be other ways of facilitating learning which are employed by deaf learners and their parents or teachers but which have not as yet been studied.

Deaf children of deaf parents, learning a sign language as their first language, do show some interesting differences from children learning a spoken language from hearing and speaking parents. Signing parents adjust their signs to increase their salience to the child, for example manipulating the child's hands, making sure that their signs are made where the child can see them, and using a variety of attention-getting devices. When interacting with babies, they help the child to divide attention between the object being named and the sign which names it, and do a lot of naming. Spoken language to deaf babies contains very much more reference to emotional content than does early signing, which tends to be highly object-oriented (which might perhaps have later repercussions for their theory of mind; Peterson & Siegal, 1995).

This use of signing for naming may be a helpful language teaching strategy. In the second year, this naming with signs is often presented with expanded movement over a larger than normal space and at a slower than usual speed; when the child attempts to copy the sign, this is typically acknowledged with a more normal form of the sign. Gallaway and Woll (1994) offer this as an instance of appropriate scaffolding in the visual modality, something that might also be done when teaching dance, for example.

The studies of interaction between children and parents in which scaffolding seems to be problematic does support, I think, the case for regarding parent–child interaction as a constituting factor in children's cognitive development. However, although there is an accumulation of evidence that children who have a good deal of sensitive child-contingent and warm scaffolding tend to do better than those who have little such experience, the association is not tremendously strong and there are clearly children who are doing well without visible scaffolding and others who are doing badly despite it. The concepts of "vulnerability" and "resilience" seem relevant here (e.g. Garmezy, 1984; Rutter, 1992), with the child's emotion regulation also being relevant (Calkins, 1994; Cole, Michel, & Teti, 1994; Field, 1994; Fox, 1994; Gardner, 1994; Thompson, 1994). Again, a great deal more research needs to be done to clarify and document what combinations of child characteristics and experience and environment are likely to lead to successful functioning or to some degree of difficulty.

As more comes to be known about individual differences in the use of language and other cognitive facilitators in interaction, it will probably become clear that there are different developmental routes, each with costs and benefits. Studies of parents' difficulties in scaffolding their children and of hard-to-scaffold children further support, I think, the case that scaffolding is a very important contributor to cognitive development. However, a great deal more research is needed in this area, not least because it may be hard to spot the different ways in which children and adults compensate for their difficulties in what I will call "conventional scaffolded learning" by developing alternatives. I will just add one note from studies of children whose achievements are prodigious (Radford, 1990). The vast majority of prodigies, cognitive, musical and sporting, have received large amounts of support and scaffolding from their parents, who in many cases concentrate all their own energies on keeping the child on task in the chosen area and on facilitating development of the child's talent. These extremes of scaffolding illustrate its effectiveness, its specificity, and in many cases its costs. Here at last there may sometimes be too much of a good thing.

CHAPTER SEVEN

Concluding remarks

I have argued that while there is a good case for regarding parent–child interaction as an important constitutive factor in the development of children's cognition, a great deal needs to be done to clarify the current description of the association between parent–child interaction and children's cognitive development, and to explain how the one affects the other. There is evidence that a high degree of child-contingent responsivity by adults is associated with comparatively advanced language, literacy, numeracy and problem-solving (and possibly also better socio-emotional development) during the preschool and primary school years, at least in mainstream Western cultures. The neo-Vygotskian model, which focuses on "scaffolding" in interactions between teacher and child, is supported by observations of children in problem-solving sessions, reading story books, simple counting, and certain manufacturing enterprises in traditional societies. Interaction which involves "scaffolding" may underlie the apparent effectiveness of some educational interventions for poor learners and disadvantaged preschool children. However, various important questions remain to be answered. For example, the demography of scaffolding, how much of it occurs in normal childrearing, is not yet adequately documented—we do not know which behaviours in which patterns are or are not functionally equivalent forms of scaffolding. We have not yet been able to dissect scaffolding into its diverse components, and establish their relative effectiveness for the various constituents of cognitive development;

indeed, it is not clear whether it would be sensible to do so, as in such a complex activity the different components may well work together in a synergistic fashion. I am happy to hypothesise that the degree to which scaffolding facilitates cognitive development depends both on the activity (with experience-dependent or culturally worked-up activities such as calculating with decimals more in need of scaffolding than experience-expectant or less culturally specific ones such as sharing objects into equal sets) and on the learner (with older and more experienced learners being more able to scaffold themselves, if they have any appropriate skills at all on entry to the new task; and also, with openness to scaffolding being a possible dimension of individual differences, some learners may stubbornly prefer to be Piagetian about learning, and insist on "doing it all my own self"); but there is a dearth of anything like systematic evidence on this. There is a fairly clear indication that a lack of anything we would recognise as scaffolding is likely to lead to development that is slower, unhappier, full of conflict, or less well suited to the requirements of participation in schooling and other cultural activities, than the development of a well-scaffolded child. However, it does not seem always to do so: research on how "resilient" children manage to avoid the effects of disadvantage may be very helpful here. We do not know whether there can be too much scaffolding, for although anecdotes about the miseries of "hot-housed" children abound, they may have been pressurised rather than scaffolded in a truly Vygotskian way. I repeat here the point made earlier, that it is not yet clear what the various components of "scaffolding" are, nor how they fit together, and therefore it is not clear how many have to be present for it to be a good, a marginal or a counter-example of "scaffolding".

We are thus in the position of thinking we know "scaffolding" or "good-for-cognition" parental behaviour when we see it, and of finding low positive correlations between a range of behaviours and a range of outcomes. There are plenty of inconsistencies in the available data, such as variations in the size and significance of correlations between what might be the same measures or what might actually be slightly different measures, or between samples that might or might not be comparable. I think they are the sorts of inconsistencies which stop the evidence gelling into a conclusive case, rather than melting it down altogether; but what is firm enough to guide me as an overloaded but conscientious parent is not firm enough to satisfy me as a would-be scientist. I believe there is enough here to help us to focus on interaction as an important contributor to development, together with the other characteristics of the participants in the interaction and the characteristics of their settings. This must be a worthy focus for practitioners, because interactions are comparatively open to modification, both for the better and for the worse.

What results can we expect from good scaffolding interaction? First, the learner learns to engage in the activity, and more generally to engage with similar learning opportunities. Second, the learner gradually acquires the skills necessary for the activity, some of which may be applicable to new tasks. Where these skills are part of the "cultural capital" required for participation in the culture, there will be effects on the individual's social acceptability and status. Third, during the course of developing the new cognitive skill, the learner may use representational redescription or similar processes to achieve an understanding of the task that is more internalised, more flexible, more automatic and more explicit than the initial representation was. Fourth, the learner learns the skills of participation in scaffolding, both as a learner and—first vicariously and then by using them as a self-scaffolding learner—as a potential teacher. Learners should come through scaffolding to take on responsibility for their own learning, perhaps to expect to be in a continual state of learning and improving their understanding and competence in a somewhat Piagetian way. Fifth, the emotional and motivational effects of scaffolding should be positive: enthusiasm and confidence towards learning tasks because of being scaffolded into successful learning; self-satisfaction and public esteem because of having acquired cultural tools; some gratitude perhaps towards the scaffolder and a feeling of being valued by them. These, I said, "should be" the effects, but not a single one is adequately documented. Much of the relevant evidence comes from studies which are focused on slightly different topics, such as the development of children who have missed out on scaffolding. The way in which an absence of scaffolding brings about a poor outcome does not show *how* the presence of scaffolding brings about a good outcome, or even that it does.

I hope that my necessarily brief account of the literature has shown that differences in the frequency and quality of scaffolding interactions between parent and child seem to be a good candidate for explaining certain differences in cognitive outcome. There are of course other candidates. "Intelligence", for example, has components which are at least initially independent of the baby's experience of social interaction with its parents; indeed, the parents are likely to be responding to the baby's alertness and attention in their interactions as scaffolders. But because it is clear that the physical development of the brain, which is seen by most intelligence theorists as at least the engine of intelligence and for many its essence, is significantly affected by the child's experience, including its experience of scaffolding, there is likely to be a bi-directional interaction between intelligence and scaffolding throughout development. Certain environmental experiences, for example chronic malnutrition and under-nutrition, may affect the child's cognition by both restricting the growth of the brain and by restricting the child's ability to explore the environment and to evoke stimulating care-taking from adults (Meadows, 1993; Puckering et al., 1995). Similarly, the cooperation of researchers from a wide range of different fields will be needed to show how it is that genetic material, beyond coding for the production of different proteins, comes to interact with the multitude of other genes and with factors beyond the genotype to have an influence on the individual's appearance and behaviour and the reactions and expectations of other genetically influenced individuals. Although genes may play a distal causal role in the development of family resemblances in cognition and personality, there is a place for parent–child interaction in the model of cognitive development as a crucial proximal variable.

The distinction between different sorts of "causes" is, I think, an important one. The philosophy of "cause" has a long and complex history. Ethologists (e.g. Hinde, 1982, 1987) distinguish between four crucial questions that are also useful to developmental psychologists, as we consider the role of parent–child interaction in cognitive development. What is the proximal cause of behaviour, the immediate stimulus which triggered it? How does the behaviour develop, what is its ontogenetic course from childhood to maturity? What is its function, what is it for? How did this behaviour evolve, how did it change during evolution?

While the ramifications of these questions are too wide to address at this point, some of their relevance to the arguments of this book is sketched, briefly, because systematic work looking at scaffolding in this framework is lacking. The proximal cause of scaffolding behaviour is clearly multiple. Parents and children are reacting to each other in scaffolding, and thus the behaviour of each is contingent on that of the other. Parents' beliefs about how to parent, their sensitivity to the child's behaviour, their resources of time, energy and knowledge, their material resources, their goodwill, and no doubt other characteristics on the one side, and the child's attributes which parallel these on the other, are all in the immediate background of the proximal cause. There will be a multiplicity of causal factors here as great as the complexity of context which, as I mentioned in Chapter 1, complicates any attempt to define what is "good" thinking. Research which documents the natural history of scaffolding, which describes when it occurs and when not, what curtails it, what maintains it, what concludes it, how it applies to different sorts of cognition, would help establish what it is and how it works.

The ontogeny of scaffolding does have a clearer theoretical formulation, though again there are gaps in the data: it is visible in adult–child interaction from the first year on, and is used in novice–expert interactions throughout life, with increasing amounts of self-scaffolding becoming possible as the learner becomes an expert learner and self-teacher. It can contribute to the acquisition of a skill at an enactive, unreflective level, as in Karmiloff-Smith's implicit representations, if the tutor presents a model for the learner's imitation; it can also contribute to the more conscious, reflective and explicit levels of representation if the scaffolder offers discussion of how and why things are done or work well, or if the learner is encouraged to reflect on the new skills and develop them further. It is perhaps particularly important for those areas where learning is largely experience-dependent and where the totality of what has to be learned has emerged too recently in evolutionary history to be coded for during evolution, for example ballet or reading; it may contribute less, perhaps, to areas where there is more experience-expectant development, for example running or simple distinctions between phonemes. Similarly, behaviour which is very much culturally specified may perhaps need more scaffolding than behaviour which varies little across cultures. Both these possibilities would go some way to helping to explain why instances of scaffolding are easier to find after infancy, when the child becomes more and more explicitly acculturated and has to integrate basic skills into more complex patterns; though the emergence of language as a channel very well suited to, or at least much used for, scaffolding would affect this too.

The question of the "function" of scaffolding is not easily dealt with, not least because the concept of "function" is perhaps as controversial as that of "cause"; but it is possible to discuss its function in terms of its results for the learner, the tutor and the wider social group, and these would seem to be positive in terms of the quality of the learning that ensues, though perhaps high in terms of the tutor's effort and time. It would also be possible to discuss the function of scaffolding as a net contributor to reproductive success; it could be that children who have been well scaffolded grow up to have more offspring whom they themselves then scaffold better so that successive generations reproduce well, but there are no data to substantiate this. This would be an extremely long-term research project, and until we have established what exactly counts as scaffolding, how it is supposed to contribute to better development, and what in fact is being learned, any data on reproductive success will be uninterpretable. It seems a reasonable bet that scaffolding, if it teaches you to be a "self-running problem-solver", can help you to surmount the challenges of life and enhance your reproductive success, via your own scaffolding of similar qualities in your offspring; but the bet is only reasonable if you're considering what is good-enough advice on how to parent, not if you wish to know what is certainly true.

The course of human evolution has been such that we would expect parent–child interaction to be immensely important for children's cognitive development, as many of the fundamental points I listed in Chapter 1 assert. Evolutionary selection has worked on our species in such a way that considerable cognitive development after birth is both necessary and possible. Various facets of evolution come together on this. Human beings have large brains in large skulls and pelvises too narrow for a large skull to pass through without damage to both mother and baby: the fetus' brain must not get too large before birth and there will therefore be considerable brain growth after it. Human beings amplify their limited sensori-motor powers with tools and therefore need complex cognitive skills for their interaction with the non-human world as tool-users and tool-makers. Human beings live in social groups and therefore need complex cognitive skills for their interaction with each other. Human beings produce small numbers of offspring, have minimally sized litters of immature and helpless babies, who therefore need a long period of being taken care of by more mature human beings. Many infant characteristics persist longer in human beings than they do in other species, a slowing-down of maturation, or "neoteny", which allows us among other things a much longer period of learning from experience and being influenced by other people. This combination of parental investment, high aptitude for learning and high demand for acquired skills, makes it seem obvious that parents' investment in interaction with their children will be developmentally important.

It seems hard to account, now, for the existence of theories which neglect this parental contribution to development. Part of the reason, I think, lies with the traditional definition of psychology as "the science of mental life", with its bias towards the study of internal mental workings in the individual, and its location of the study of "individual differences" in the limited fields of intelligence, personality and psychopathology. Part also has to do with the influence of Piaget's work, where the version that has influenced English-language psychology focused on universal cognitive acquisitions, processes and structures, and said so little about social interaction that its neglect if anything intensified. Defining cognition in terms of coolness, rationality, and internally generated initiatives, monitoring and correction, and ignoring its costs, followed also from the information-processing analogy with computers. These approaches have achieved a great deal (and developments such as connectionism may do a great deal more), but the picture they build up systematically lacks attention to our learning from others: learning that is so pervasive that it has been underestimated, so complex that we can only begin to describe it, so multi-faceted that we do not know how much of what sort has what benefits and what costs. Sociologists (e.g. Mayall, 1994) have rightly complained about the narrow individualism of much developmental psychology, though their criticisms often betray a distinctly limited acquaintance with the subject. Recognition of concepts such as "cultural capital" and pupils' resources for learning (Pollard, 1995) might enrich the developmental psychology of cognition. The development of children's thinking clearly does not proceed in an unemotional value-free vacuum. They are surrounded by other members of the species who have a vested interest in their learning, who will seek to improve it, acculturate it, constrain it, assess it and reward it in due degree; and the child internalises at least some of these social pressures and expectations while maintaining other "interests-at-hand", such as having fun and not losing face. Theories that edit out this complexity can only go a limited distance towards understanding cognitive development. Both for the future of psychology and for the better management of children's development, we must work towards an understanding which is both wider and more precise.

References

Aber, J.L. (1994). Poverty, violence, and child development: Untangling family and community level effects. In C.A. Nelson (Ed.), *Threats to optimal development: Integrating biological, psychological and social risk factors.* Minnesota Symposium on Child Psychology Vol. 27. Hillsdale, NJ: Lawrence Erlbaum Associates Inc.

Aber, J.L., Allen, J.P., Carlson, V., & Cicchetti, D. (1989). The effects of maltreatment on development during early childhood: Recent studies and their theoretical, clinical, and policy implications. In D. Cicchetti & V. Carlson (Eds.), *Child maltreatment: Theory and research on the causes and consequences of child abuse and neglect.* Cambridge: Cambridge University Press.

Alper, J.S., & Natowicz, M.R. (1992). The allure of genetic explanations. *British Medical Journal, 305,* 666.

Anderson, M. (1992). *Intelligence and cognitive development.* Oxford: Blackwell.

Aslin, R.N., Pisoni, D.B., Jusczyk, P.W. (1983). Auditory speech perception in infancy. In M.M. Haith & J.J. Campos (Eds.), *Handbook of child psychology.* New York: Wiley.

Barrett, M., Harris, M., & Chasin, J. (1991). Early lexical development and maternal speech: A comparison of children's initial and subsequent uses of words. *Journal of Child Language, 18,* 21–40.

Barton, M.E. (1994). The rest of the family: The role of fathers and siblings in early language development. In C. Gallaway & B.J. Richards (Eds.), *Input and interaction in language acquisition.* Cambridge: Cambridge University Press.

Bates, E.A., & Elman, J.L. (1993). Connectionism and the study of change. In M. Johnson (Ed.), *Brain development and cognition.* Oxford: Blackwell.

Bates, E., Bretherton, I., & Snyder, L. (1988). *From first words to grammar: Individual differences and dissociable mechanisms.* New York: Cambridge University Press.

Bates, E., Dale, P.S., & Thal, D. (1995). Individual differences and their implications for theories of language development. In P. Fletcher & B. MacWhinney (Eds.), *The handbook of child language*. Oxford: Blackwell.

Baumrind, D. (1993). The average expectable environment is not good enough. *Child Development, 64*, 1299–1317.

Bechtel, W., & Abrahamsen, A. (1991). *Connectionism and the mind: An introduction to parallel processing*. Oxford: Blackwell.

Bergeman, C.S., & Plomin, R. (1988). Parental mediators of the genetic relationship between home environment and infant mental development. *British Journal of Developmental Psychology, 6*, 11–19.

Bergeman, C.S., & Plomin, R. (1989). Genotype–environment interaction. In M.H. Bornstein & J.S. Bruner (Eds.), *Interaction in human development*. Hillsdale, NJ: Lawrence Erlbaum Associates Inc.

Berrueta-Clermont, J.R. (1984). *Changed lives: The effects of the Perry Preschool Program on youths through age 19*. Ypsilanti: High/Scope Press.

Bettes, B. (1988). Maternal depression and motherese: Temporal and intonational features. *Child Development, 59*, 1089–1096.

Bishop, D., & Mogford, K. (Eds.) (1993). *Language development in exceptional circumstances*. Hove: Lawrence Erlbaum Associates Ltd.

Blake, J. (1989). *Family size and achievement*. Berkeley, CA: University of California Press.

Blank, M. (1973). *Teaching learning in the preschool: A dialogue approach*. Columbus, OH: Charles Merrill.

Blank, M., Rose, S.A., & Berlin, L.J. (1978). *The language of learning*. New York: Grune & Stratton.

Bornstein, M., & Bruner, J. (Eds.) (1989). *Interaction in human development*. Hillsdale, NJ: Lawrence Erlbaum Associates Inc.

Bouchard, T.J. (1993). The genetic architecture of human intelligence. In P.A. Vernon (Ed.), *Biological approaches to the study of human intelligence*. Norwood, NJ: Ablex.

Bouchard, T.J. (1994). Genes, environment, and personality. *Science, 264*, 1700–1701.

Bovet, M., Parrat-Dayan, S., & Voneche, J. (1989). Cognitive development and interaction. In M.H. Bornstein & J. Bruner (Eds.), *Interaction in human development*. Hillsdale, NJ: Lawrence Erlbaum Associates Inc.

Bradley, R. (1994). The HOME Inventory: Review and reflections. In H.W. Reese (Ed.), *Advances in child development and behaviour*, Vol. 25. San Diego, CA: Academic Press.

Bradley, R., & Caldwell, B. (1980). The relation of the home environment, cognitive competence, and IQ among males and females. *Child Development, 51*, 1140–1148.

Bradley, R., & Caldwell, B. (1984). 174 children: A study of the relationship between home environment and cognitive development during the first five years. In A.W. Gottfried (Ed.), *Home environment and early cognitive development*. New York: Academic Press.

Bradley, R., & Caldwell, B.M. (1995). Caregiving and the regulation of child growth and development: Describing proximal aspects of caregiving systems. *Developmental Review, 15*, 38–85.

Bradley, R., Caldwell, B., & Rock, S. (1988). Home environment and school performance: A ten year follow-up and examination of three models of environmental action. *Child Development, 59*, 852–867.

Bradley, R., Caldwell, B., Rock, S., Ramey, C., Barnard, K., Gray, C., Hammond, M., Mitchell, S., Gottfried, S., Siegel, L., & Johnson, D. (1989). Home environment and cognitive development in the first three years of life: A collaborative study involving six sites and three ethnic groups in North America. *Developmental Psychology, 25*, 217–235.

Breznitz, Z., & Sherman, T. (1987). Speech patterning of natural discourse of well and depressed mothers and their young children. *Child Development, 58*, 395–400.

Broman, S., Nichols, P.L., Shaughnessy, P., & Kennedy, W. (1987). *Retardation in young children: A developmental study of cognitive deficits.* Hillsdale, NJ: Lawrence Erlbaum Associates Inc.

Bronfenbrenner, U. (1979). *The ecology of human development.* Cambridge, MA: Harvard University Press.

Bronfenbrenner, U. (1986). Ecology of the family as a context for human development. *Developmental Psychology, 22*, 723–742.

Bronfenbrenner, U., & Ceci, S. (1993). Heredity, environment and the question "How". In R. Plomin & J. McClearn (Eds.), *Nature, nurture and psychology.* Washington, DC: American Psychological Association.

Bronfenbrenner, U., & Ceci, S. (1994). Nature–nurture reconceptualized in developmental perspective: A bioecological model. *Psychological Review, 101*, 568–586.

Brophy, J. (1986). Teacher influences on student achievement. *American Psychologist, 41*, 1069–1077.

Brophy, J., & Good, T. (1986). Teacher behaviour and student achievement. In M. Wittrock (Ed.), *Third handbook of research on teaching.* New York: Macmillan.

Brown, A.L., & Campione, J.C. (1986). Psychological theory and the study of learning. *American Psychologist, 41*, 1059–1068.

Brown, A.L., & Campione, J.C. (1988). Communities of learning and thinking: or a context by any other name. *Contributions to Human Development, 21*, 108–126.

Brown, A.L., & Palincsar, A.S. (1989). Guided, co-operative learning and individual knowledge acquisition. In L.B. Resnick (Ed.), *Knowing, learning and instruction.* Hillsdale, NJ: Lawrence Erlbaum Associates Inc.

Brown, A.L., Bransford, J.D., Ferrara, R.A., & Campione, J.C. (1983). Learning, remembering and understanding. In J.H. Flavell & E.M. Markman (Eds.), *Handbook of child psychology*, Vol. 3. New York: John Wiley.

Brown, A.L., Palincsar, A.S., & Armbruster, B.B. (1984). Instructing comprehension fostering activities in interactive learning situations. In H. Mandl, N. Stein, & T. Trabasso (Eds.), *Learning and comprehension of texts.* Hillsdale, NJ: Lawrence Erlbaum Associates Inc.

Brown, G.W., & Harris, T. (1978). *Social origins of depression.* London: Tavistock.

Bruner, J. (1990). *Acts of meaning.* Cambridge, MA: Harvard University Press.

Bryant, P.E. (1995). Children and arithmetic. *Journal of Child Psychology and Psychiatry, 36*, 3–32.

Bryant, P.E., & Bradley, L. (1985). *Children's reading problems.* Oxford: Blackwell.

Byne, W. (1994). The biological evidence challenged. *Science, 262*, 578–580.

Calkins, S.D. (1994). Origins and outcomes of differences in emotion regulation. In N.A. Fox (Ed.), *The development of emotion regulation*. Monographs of the Society for Research in Child Development Vol. 59. Chicago, IL: University of Chicago Press.

Campbell, S.B. (1995). Behaviour problems in preschool children: A review of recent research. *Journal of Child Psychology and Psychiatry, 36*, 113–150.

Capron, C., & Duyme, M. (1989). Assessment of effects of socio-economic status on IQ in a full cross-fostering study. *Nature, 340*, 552–554.

Cardon, L.R. (1994). Specific cognitive ability. In J.C. DeFries, R. Plomin, & D.W. Fulker (Eds.), *Nature and nurture during middle childhood*. Cambridge, MA: Blackwell.

Cardon, L.R., Fulker, D.W., DeFries, J.C., & Plomin, R. (1992). Continuity and change in general cognitive ability from 1–7 years of age. *Developmental Psychology, 28*, 64–73.

Carr, J. (1988). Six weeks to twenty-one years old: A longitudinal study of children with Down's syndrome and their families. *Journal of Child Psychology and Psychiatry, 29*, 407–431.

Carraher, T.N., Carraher, D.W., & Schliemann, A.D. (1985). Mathematics in the street and in school. *British Journal of Developmental Psychology, 3*, 21–29.

Chapman, R.S. (1995). Language development in children and adolescents with Down's syndrome. In P. Fletcher & B. MacWhinney (Eds.), *The handbook of child language*. Oxford: Blackwell.

Cherny, S.S., & Cardon, L.R. (1994). General cognitive ability. In J.C. DeFries, R. Plomin, & D.W. Fulker (Eds.), *Nature and nurture during middle childhood*. Cambridge, MA: Blackwell.

Cicchetti, D. (1994). Integrating developmental risk factors: Perspectives from developmental psychopathology. In C.A. Nelson (Ed.), *Threats to optimal development: Integrating biological, psychological and social risk factors*. Minnesota Symposium on Child Psychology Vol. 27. Hillsdale, NJ: Lawrence Erlbaum Associates Inc.

Clark, A. (1989). *Microcognition: Philosophy, cognitive science, and parallel distributed processing*. Cambridge, MA: MIT Press.

Clark, M. (1976). *Young fluent readers*. London: Heinemann.

Clark, M. (1988). *Children under five: Educational research and evidence*. London: Gordon and Breach.

Clarke-Stewart, A. (1994). *Children at home and in daycare*. Hove: Lawrence Erlbaum Associates Ltd.

Cogill, S.R., Caplan, H.L., Alexandra, H., Robson, K.M., & Kumar, R. (1986). Impact of maternal depression on cognitive development of young children. *British Medical Journal, 292*, 1165–1167.

Cohler, B.J., Grunebaum, H.U., Weiss, J.L., Gamer, E., & Gallant, D.H. (1977). Disturbance of attention among schizophrenic, depressed and well mothers and their young children. *Journal of Child Psychology and Psychiatry, 18*, 115–135.

Cole, M. (1990). Cognitive development and formal schooling: The evidence from cross-cultural research. In L.C. Moll (Ed.), *Vygotsky and education*. Cambridge: Cambridge University Press.

Cole, P.M., Michel, M.K., & Teti, L.O'D. (1994). The development of emotion regulation and dysregulation: A clinical perspective. In N.A. Fox (Ed.), *The development of emotion regulation*. Monographs of the Society for Research in Child Development Vol. 59. Chicago, IL: University of Chicago Press.

Consortium for Longitudinal Studies (1983). *As the twig is bent*. London: Lawrence Erlbaum Associates Ltd.

Conti-Ramsden, G. (1994). Language interaction with atypical learners. In C. Gallaway & B.J. Richards (Eds.), *Input and interaction in language acquisition*. Cambridge: Cambridge University Press.

Cooke, R. (1994). Factors affecting survival and outcome at three years in extremely preterm infants. *Archives of Disease in Childhood, 71*, 28–31.

Cox, A.D., Puckering, C., Pound, A., & Mills, M. (1987). The impact of maternal depression in young children. *Journal of Child Psychology and Psychiatry, 28*, 917–928.

Cox, M.V. (Ed.) (1980). *Are young children egocentric?* London: Batsford.

Coyne, J.C., & Downey, G. (1991). Social factors and psychopathology: Stress, social support and coping processes. *Annual Review of Psychology, 42*, 401–425.

Cromer, R.F. (1991). *The cognition hypothesis of language acquisition? From language and thought in normal and handicapped children*. Oxford: Blackwell.

Cummings, E.M., & Davies, P.T. (1994). Maternal development and child adjustment. *Journal of Child Psychology and Psychiatry, 35*, 73–112.

Davies, P.T., & Cummings, E.M. (1994). Marital conflict and child adjustment: An emotional security hypothesis. *Psychological Bulletin, 116*, 387–411.

DeFries, J.C., Plomin, R., & Fulker, D.W. (1994). *Nature and nurture in middle childhood*. Oxford: Blackwell.

Dix, T. (1991). The affective organisation of parenting: Adaptive and maladaptive processes. *Psychological Bulletin, 110*, 3–25.

Doise, W., & Mugny, G. (1984). *The social development of the intellect*. Oxford: Pergamon Press.

Downey, G., & Coyne, J.C. (1990). Children of depressed parents: An integrative review. *Psychological Bulletin, 108*, 50–76.

Dunn, J. (1988). *The beginnings of social understanding*. Oxford: Blackwell.

Dunn, J. (1993). *Young children's close relationships: Beyond attachment*. Newbury Park, CA: Sage.

Dunn, J., & McGuire, S. (1994). Young children's shared experiences: A summary of studies in Cambridge and Colorado. In E.M. Hetherington, D. Reiss, & R. Plomin (Eds.), *Separate social worlds of siblings: Impact of nonshared environment on development*. Hillsdale, NJ: Lawrence Erlbaum Associates Inc.

Dunning, D.B., Mason, J., & Stewart, J.P. (1994). Reading to preschoolers: A response to Scarborough and Dobrich and recommendations for future research. *Developmental Review, 14*, 324–329.

Duyme, M. (1988). School success and social class: An adoption study. *Developmental Psychology, 24*, 203–209.

Duyme, M. (1990). Antisocial behaviour and post-natal environment: A French adoption study. *Journal of Child Psychology and Psychiatry, 31*, 699–710.

Edelman, G. (1994). *Bright air, brilliant fire: On the matter of the mind*. Harmondsworth: Penguin.

Ely, R., & Gleason, B. (1995). Socialisation across contexts. In P. Fletcher & B. MacWhinney (Eds.), *The handbook of child language*. Oxford: Blackwell.

Erickson, M.F., Egeland, B., & Pianta, R. (1989). The effects of maltreatment on the development of young children. In D. Cicchetti & V. Carlson (Eds.), *Child maltreatment: Theory and research on the causes and consequences of child abuse and neglect*. Cambridge: Cambridge University Press.

Escobar, G.J., Littenberg, B., & Pettiti, D.B. (1991). Outcome among surviving very low birthweight infants: A meta-analysis. *Archives of Disease in Childhood, 66*, 204–211.

Eysenck, H.J. (1971). *Race, intelligence and education*. London: Temple Smith.

Eysenck, H.J. (1986). The theory of intelligence and the psychophysiology of cognition. In R.J. Sternberg (Ed.), *Advances in the psychology of human intelligence*, Vol. 3. Hillsdale, NJ: Lawrence Erlbaum Associates Inc.

Eysenck, H.J. (1993). The biological basis of intelligence. In P.A.Vernon (Ed.), *Biological approaches to the study of human intelligence*. Norwood, NJ: Ablex.

Farrar, M.J. (1990). Discourse and the acquisition of grammatical morphemes. *Journal of Child Language, 17*, 607–624.

Field, T. (1994). The effects of mother's physical and emotional unavailability on emotion regulation. In N.A. Fox (Ed.), *The development of emotion regulation*. Monographs of the Society for Research in Child Development Vol. 59. Chicago, IL: University of Chicago Press.

Fischer, K.W., & Bidell, T. (1991). Constraining nativist inferences about cognitive capacities. In S. Carey & R. Gelman (Eds.), *The epigenesis of mind*. Hove: Lawrence Erlbaum Associates Ltd.

Flynn, J.R. (1987). Massive IQ gains in 14 nations: What IQ tests really measure. *Psychological Bulletin, 101*, 171–191.

Fodor, J. A. (1981). *Representations: Philosophical essays on the foundations of cognitive science*. Brighton: Harvester.

Fodor, J.A. (1983). *The modularity of mind*. Cambridge, MA: MIT Press.

Forman, E.A., Minick, N., & Stone, C.A. (1993). *Contexts for learning: Sociocultural dynamics in children's development*. New York: Oxford University Press.

Fox, N.A. (Ed.) (1994). *The development of emotion regulation*. Monographs of the Society for Research in Child Development Vol. 59. Chicago, IL: University of Chicago Press.

Fraser, B.J. (1989). Research syntheses on school and instructional effectiveness. *International Journal of Educational Research, 13*, 707–719.

Freund, L.S. (1990). Maternal regulation of children's problem-solving behaviour and its impact on children's performance. *Child Development, 61*, 113–126.

Fujinaga, T., Kasuga, T., Uchida, N., & Saiga, H. (1990). *Long-term follow-up study of children developmentally retarded by early environmental deprivation*. Genetic, Social and General Psychology Monographs Vol. 116. Washington, DC: Heldref Publications.

Furrow, D., Moore, C., Davidge, J., & Chiasson, L. (1992). Mental terms in mothers' and childrens' speech—similarities and relationships. *Journal of Child Language, 19*, 617–631.

Furrow, D., Nelson, K., & Benedict, H. (1979). Mothers' speech to children and syntactic development: Some simple relationships. *Journal of Child Language, 6*, 423–442.

Gallaway, C., & Woll, B.J. (1994). Interaction and childhood deafness. In C. Gallaway & B.J. Richards (Eds.), *Input and interaction in language acquisition*. Cambridge: Cambridge University Press.

Garber, R. (1988). *The Milwaukee Project: Preventing mental retardation in children at risk*. Washington, DC: American Association on Mental Retardation.

Garber, R., & Hodge, D. (1989). Risk for deceleration in the rate of mental development. *Developmental Review, 9,* 259–300.

Gardner, F. (1994). The quality of joint activity between mothers and their children with behaviour problems. *Journal of Child Psychology and Psychiatry, 35,* 935–948.

Garmezy, N. (1984). Stress-resistant children: The search for protective factors. In J.E. Stevenson (Ed.), *Recent research in developmental psychopathology.* Oxford: Pergamon Press.

Garton, A. (1992). *Social interaction and the development of language and cognition.* Hove: Lawrence Erlbaum Associates Ltd.

Gelman, R. (1990). First principles organise attention to and learning about relevant data: Number and the animate–inanimate distinction as examples. *Cognitive Science, 14,* 79–106.

Gelman, R., & Gallistel, R. (1978). *The child's understanding of number.* Cambridge, MA: Harvard University Press.

Gelman, R., & Meck, E. (1983). Preschoolers' counting: Principles before skill. *Cognition, 13,* 343–359.

Glassman, M. (1994). All things being equal: The two roads of Piaget and Vygotsky. *Developmental Review, 14,* 186–214.

Goldfarb, W. (1945). Effects of psychological deprivation in infancy and subsequent stimulation. *American Journal of Psychiatry, 102,* 18–33.

Goldin-Meadow, S., & Mylander, C. (1990). The role of parental input in the development of a morphological system. *Journal of Child Language, 17,* 527–563.

Goldsmith, D.F., & Rogoff, B. (1995). Sensitivity and teaching by dysphoric and nondysphoric women in structured versus unstructured situations. *Developmental Psychology, 31,* 388–394.

Goswami, U. (1992). *Analogical reasoning in children.* Hove: Lawrence Erlbaum Associates Ltd.

Goswami, U., & Bryant, P. (1990). *Phonological skills and learning to read.* Hove: Lawrence Erlbaum Associates Ltd.

Gottfried, A.E., & Gottfried, A.W. (1984). Home environment and mental development in middle-class children in the first three years. In A.W. Gottfried (Ed.), *Environment and early cognitive development: Longitudinal research.* New York: Academic Press.

Gottlieb, G. (1983). The psychobiological approach to developmental issues. In M.M. Haith & J.J. Campos (Eds.), *Handbook of child psychology,* Vol. 2. New York: John Wiley.

Gottlieb, G. (1991). Experiential canalization of behavioural development: Theory. *Developmental Psychology, 27,* 4–13.

Gould, S.J. (1984). *The mismeasure of man.* Harmondsworth, UK: Penguin.

Greenough, W.T. (1986). What's special about development? Thoughts on the basis of experience-sensitive synaptic plasticity. In W.T. Greenough & J.M. Juraska (Eds.), *Developmental neuropsychology.* New York: Academic Press.

Greenough, W.T. (1991). Experience as a component of normal development: Evolutionary considerations. *Developmental Psychology, 27,* 14–17.

Greenough, W.T., & Black, J.E. (1992). Induction of brain structure by experience: Substrates for cognitive development. In M. Gunnar & C.A. Nelson (Eds.), *Developmental behavioural neuroscience*: Minnesota Symposium on Child Psychology Vol. 24. Hillsdale, NJ: Lawrence Erlbaum Associates Inc.

Greenough,W.T., Black, J.E., & Wallace, C.S. (1987). Experience and brain development. *Child Development, 58*, 539–559.

Gunn, P. (1985). Speech and language. In D. Lane & B. Stratford (Eds.), *Current approaches to Down's syndrome*. London: Holt, Rinehart and Winston.

Hammen, C., Burge, D., & Stansbury, K. (1990). Relationship of mother and child variables to child outcomes in a high-risk sample: A causal modelling analysis. *Developmental Psychology, 26*, 24–30.

Hammen, C., Gordon, D., Burge, D., Adrian, C., Jaenicke, C., & Hiroto, D. (1987). Maternal affective disorders, illness and stress: Risk for children's psychopathology. *American Journal of Psychiatry, 144*, 736–741.

Hampson, J., & Nelson, K. (1993). The relation of maternal language to variation in rate and style of language acquisition. *Journal of Child Language, 20*, 313–342.

Harris, M. (1992). *Language experience and early language development: From input to uptake*. Hove: Lawrence Erlbaum Associates Ltd.

Harris, M., Barrett, M., Jones, D., & Brookes, S. (1988). Linguistic input and early word meaning. *Journal of Child Language, 15*, 77–94

Harris, M., Jones, D., Brookes, S., & Grant, J. (1986). Relations between the nonverbal context of maternal speech and rate of language development. *British Journal of Developmental Psychology, 4*, 261–268.

Hartup, W.W., & van Lieshout, C.F.M. (1995). Personality development in social context. *Annual Review of Psychology, 46*, 655–687.

Heath, S.B. (1983). *Ways with words*. Cambridge: Cambridge University Press.

Heath, S.B. (1986). What no bedtime story means: Narrative skills at home and at school. In B. Schieffelin & E. Ochs (Eds.), *Language socialisation across cultures*. Cambridge: Cambridge University Press.

Heath, S.B. (1989). The learner as cultural member. In M.L. Rice & R.L. Schiefelbusch (Eds.), *Teachability of language*. Baltimore, MD: Brooks.

Heckhausen, J. (1987). Balancing for weakness and challenging developmental potential: A longitudinal study of mother–infant dyads in apprenticeship interactions. *Developmental Psychology, 23*, 762–770.

Hess, R.D., & Shipman, V.C. (1965). Early experience and the socialisation of cognitive modes in children. *Child Development, 36*, 869–886.

Hiester, M., Ogawa, J.R., Ostoja, E., Susman, A., & Weinfield, N.S. (1994). The role of biological and psychosocial risk factors in development. In C.A. Nelson (Ed.), *Threats to optimal development: Integrating biological, psychological and social risk factors*. Minnesota Symposium on Child Psychology Vol. 27. Hillsdale, NJ: Lawrence Erlbaum Associates Inc.

Hinde, R.A. (1982). *Ethology*. London: Fontana.

Hinde, R.A. (1987). *Individuals, relationship and culture: Links between ethology and the social sciences*. Cambridge: Cambridge University Press.

Hodapp, R.M., Goldfield, E.G., & Boyatzis, C.J. (1984). The use and effectiveness of maternal scaffolding in mother–infant games. *Child Development, 59*, 1387–1396.

Hoff-Ginsberg, E. (1990). Maternal speech and the child's development of syntax: A further look. *Journal of Child Language, 17*, 85–99.

Hoffman, L. (1991). The influence of the family environment on personality: Accounting for sibling differences. *Psychological Bulletin, 110*, 187–203.

Howes, C. (1988). Relations between early child care and schooling. *Developmental Psychology, 24*, 53–75.

Howes, C. (1990). Can the age of entry into child care and the quality of child care predict adjustment in kindergarten? *Developmental Psychology, 26,* 292–303.

Hulme, C. (1987). Reading retardation. In J.R. Beech & A.M. Colley (Eds.), *Cognitive approaches to reading.* Chichester: John Wiley.

Humphrey, N. (1976). The social function of intellect. In P. Bateson & R. Hinde (Eds.), *Growing points in ethology.* Cambridge: Cambridge University Press.

Humphrey, N. (1983). *Consciousness regained: Chapters in the development of the mind.* Oxford: Oxford University Press.

Huston, A. (Ed.) (1991). *Children and poverty: Child development and public policy.* New York: Cambridge University Press.

Jackson, J.F. (1993). Human behavioural genetics, Scarr's theory, and her views on interventions: A critical review and commentary on their implications for African American children. *Child Development, 64,* 1318–1332.

Jacobvitz, D., & Sroufe, A. (1987). The early caregiver–child relationship and attention-deficit disorder with hyperactivity in kindergarten: A prospective study. *Child Development, 58,* 1496–1504.

Jencks, C. (1975). *Inequality: A reassessment of the effects of family and schooling.* Harmondsworth: Penguin.

Jensen, A.R. (1969). *Environment, heredity and intelligence.* Cambridge, MA: Harvard Educational Review.

Jensen, A.R. (1989). Raising IQ without raising g? A review of "The Milwaukee Project: Preventing mental retardation in children at risk". *Developmental Review, 9,* 234–258.

Jensen, A.R., & Sinha, S.N. (1993). Physiological correlates of human intelligence. In P.A. Vernon (Ed.), *Biological approaches to the study of human intelligence.* Norwood, NJ: Ablex.

Johnson, A., Townsend, P., Yudkin, P., Bull, D., & Wilkinson, A.R. (1993). Functional abilities at age 4 years of children born before 29 weeks gestation. *British Medical Journal, 306,* 1715–1718.

Johnson, M. (Ed.) (1993). *Brain development and cognition.* Oxford: Blackwell.

Jones, O.H.M. (1979). A comparative study of mother–child communication with Down's syndrome and normal infants. In D. Shaffer & J. Dunn (Eds.), *The first year of life.* Chichester: John Wiley.

Jowett, S., & Sylva, K. (1986). Does kind of pre-school matter? *Educational Research, 28,* 21–31.

Kaler, S.R., & Freeman, B.J. (1994). Analysis of environmental deprivation: Cognition and social development in Romanian orphans. *Journal of Child Psychology and Psychiatry, 35,* 769–782.

Karmiloff-Smith, A. (1991). Beyond modularity: Innate constraints and developmental change. In S. Carey & R. Gelman (Eds.), *The epigenesis of mind.* Hove: Lawrence Erlbaum Associates Ltd.

Karmiloff-Smith, A. (1992). *Beyond modularity: A developmental perspective on cognitive science.* Cambridge, MA: Bradford.

Karmiloff-Smith, A. (1994). Precis of beyond modularity: A developmental perspective on cognitive science. *Behavioural and Brain Sciences, 17,* 693–745.

Karmiloff-Smith, A., & Inhelder, B. (1974–75). If you want to get ahead, get a theory. *Cognition, 3,* 195–212.

Knutson, J.F. (1995). Psychological characteristics of maltreated children: Putative risk factors and consequences. *Annual Review of Psychology, 46,* 401–431.

Kontos, S. (1983). Adult–child interaction and the development of metacognition. *Journal of Educational Research, 77*, 43–64.

Kozulin, A. (1990). *Vygotsky's psychology*. Brighton: Harvester.

Lave, J. (1988). *Cognition in practice*. Cambridge: Cambridge University Press.

Lazar, I., & Darlington, R. (1982). The lasting effects of early education: A report from the Consortium of Longitudinal Studies. *Journal of the Society for Research into Child Development, 47* (2–3).

Lee, S., Stigler, J.W., & Schnur, E. (1988). Does Head Start work? A 1-year follow-up comparison of disadvantaged children attending Head Start, no preschool, and other preschool programs. *Developmental Psychology, 24*, 210–222.

Lieven, E.M. (1994). Crosslinguistic and crosscultural aspects of language addressed to children. In C. Gallaway & B.J. Richards (Eds.), *Input and interaction in language acquisition*. Cambridge: Cambridge University Press.

Light, P.H. (1979). *The development of social sensitivity*. Cambridge: Cambridge University Press.

Loehlin, J. (1987). Twin studies, environment differences, age changes. *Behavioural and Brain Sciences, 10*, 30–31.

Loehlin, J. (1992). *Genes and environment in personality development*. Thousand Oaks, CA: Sage.

Lonigan, C. (1994). Reading to preschoolers exposed: Is the emperor really naked? *Developmental Review, 14*, 303–323.

Luster, T., & Dubow, E. (1992). Home environment and maternal intelligence: A comparison of preschool and school-age children. *Merrill-Palmer Quarterly, 38*, 151–175.

Lynn, R. (1993). Nutrition and intelligence. In P.A.Vernon (Ed.), *Biological approaches to the study of human intelligence*. Norwood, NJ: Ablex.

Maccoby, E.E., & Martin, J.A. (1983). Socialization in the context of the family: Parent–child interaction. In E.M. Hetherington (Ed.), *Handbook of child psychology*, Vol. 4. New York: John Wiley.

Macfarlane, D. (1987). *Oxford companion to animal behaviour*. Oxford: Oxford University Press.

Maddox, J. (1993). Wilful public misunderstanding of genetics. *Nature, 364*, 281.

Marjoribanks, K. (1979). *Families and their learning environments: An empirical analysis*. London: Routledge.

Marjoribanks, K. (1994). Families, schools and children's learning: A study of children's learning environments. *International Journal of Educational Research, 21*, 439–555.

Markova, I. (1982). *Paradigms, thought and language*. Chichester: John Wiley.

Maughan, B. (1995). Long-term outcomes of developmental reading problems. *Journal of Child Psychology and Psychiatry, 36*, 357–372.

Mayall, B. (Ed.) (1994). *Children's childhood: Observed and experienced*. London: Falmer Press.

McCabe, A.E. (1989). Differential language learning styles in young children: The importance of context. *Developmental Review, 9*, 1–20.

McCartney, K., Harris, M.J., & Bernieri, F. (1990). Growing up and growing apart: A developmental meta-analysis of twin studies. *Psychological Bulletin, 107*, 226–237.

McGue, M. (1994). Why developmental psychology should find room for behavioural genetics. In C.A. Nelson (Ed.), *Threats to optimal development: Integrating biological, psychological and social risk factors*. Minnesota Symposium on Child Psychology Vol. 27. Hillsdale, NJ: Lawrence Erlbaum Associates Inc.

McLeish, J. (1991). *Number*. London: Bloomsbury.

McNaughton, S., & Leyland, J. (1990). The shifting focus of maternal tutoring across different difficulty levels on a problem-solving task. *British Journal of Developmental Psychology, 8*, 147–155.

Meadows, S. (1983). *Developing thinking*. London: Routledge.

Meadows, S. (1986). *Understanding child development*. London: Hutchinson.

Meadows, S. (1993). *The child as thinker*. London: Routledge.

Meadows, S., & Cashdan, A. (1988). *Helping children learn: Contributions to a cognitive curriculum*. London: David Fulton.

Meadows, S., & Mills, M.P. (1987). *Preschool parenting style and children's cognition: Follow-up on starting school*. End of Grant Report to ESRC on Project C002320101.

Mills, A. (1993). Visual handicap. In D. Bishop & K. Mogford (Eds.), *Language development in exceptional circumstances*. Hove: Lawrence Erlbaum Associates Ltd.

Mills, M., & Funnell, E. (1983). Experience and cognitive processing. In S. Meadows (Ed.), *Developing thinking*. London: Methuen.

Mills, M.P., Puckering, C., Pound, A., & Cox, A. (1985). What is it about depressed mothers that affects their children's functioning? In J. Stevenson (Ed.), *Recent advances in developmental psychopathology*. Oxford: Pergamon Press.

Minsky, M. (1988). *The society of mind*. New York: Simon and Schuster.

Mogford, K. (1993). Oral language acquisition in the pre-linguistically deaf. In D. Bishop & K. Mogford (Eds.), *Language development in exceptional circumstances*. Hove: Lawrence Erlbaum Associates Ltd.

Morss, J. (1985). Early cognitive development: Difference or delay? In D. Lane & B. Stratford (Eds.), *Current approaches to Down's syndrome*. London: Holt, Rinehart and Winston.

Mortimore, P., Sammons, P., Stoll, L., Lewis, D., & Ecob, R. (1988). *School matters: The junior school years*. Wells: Open Books.

Mortimore, P., Sammons, P., Stoll, L., Lewis, D., & Ecob, R. (1989). A study of effective junior schools. *International Journal of Educational Research, 13*, 753–768.

Murray, A.D., Johnson, J., & Peters, J. (1990). Fine-tuning of utterance length to preverbal infants: Effects on later language development. *Journal of Child Language, 17*, 511–525.

Neiderhiser, J.M. (1994). Family environment in early childhood, outcomes in middle childhood, and genetic mediation. In J.C. DeFries, R. Plomin, & D.W. Fulker (Eds.), *Nature and nurture during middle childhood*. Cambridge, MA: Blackwell.

Nolen-Hoeksma, S., Mumme, D., Wolfson, A., & Guskin, K. (1995). Helplessness in children of depressed and nondepressed mothers. *Developmental Psychology, 31*, 377–387.

Nunes, T. (1992). Cognitive invariants and cultural variation in mathematical concepts. *International Journal of Behaviour Development, 15*, 433–453.

Nunes, T., Schliemann, A.D., & Carraher, D. (1993). *Street mathematics and school mathematics*. New York: Cambridge University Press.

Ochs, E., & Schieffelin, B. (Eds.) (1986). *Language socialisation across cultures*. New York: Cambridge University Press.

Ochs, E., & Schieffelin, B. (1995). The impact of language socialisation on grammatical development. In P. Fletcher & B. MacWhinney (Eds.), *The handbook of child language*. Oxford: Blackwell.

Osborn, A., & Milbank, J. (1987). *The effects of early education*. Oxford: Clarendon Press.

Pellegrini, A.D., Perlmutter, J.C., Galda, L., & Brody, G.H. (1990). Joint reading between black Head Start children and their mothers. *Child Development, 61*, 443–453.

Perret-Clermont, A.-N., & Brossard, A. (1985). On the interdigitation of social and cognitive processes. In R.A. Hinde, A.N. Perret-Clermont, & J. Stevenson-Hinde (Eds.), *Social relationships and cognitive development*. Oxford: Clarendon Press.

Peterson, C.C., & Siegal, M. (1995). Deafness, conversation and theory of mind. *Journal of Child Psychology and Psychiatry, 36*, 459–474.

Peterson, S.E., Fow, P.T., Snyder, A., & Raichle, M.E. (1990). Activation of extrastriate and frontal cortical areas by visual words and word-like stimuli. *Science, 249*, 1041–1044.

Piaget, J. (1932). *The moral judgement of the child*. Harmondsworth: Penguin.

Piaget, J. (1962). Comments on Vygotsky's critical remarks. *Archives de Psychologie, 183*, 237–249.

Piaget, J. (1968). *Six psychological studies*. London: University of London Press.

Piaget, J. (1978). *The development of thought: Equilibration of cognitive structures*. Oxford: Blackwell.

Piaget, J. (1983). Piaget's theory. In W. Kessen (Ed.), *Handbook of child psychology*, Vol. 1. New York: John Wiley.

Pine, J. (1994). The language of primary caregivers. In C. Gallaway & B.J. Richards (Eds.), *Input and interaction in language acquisition*. Cambridge: Cambridge University Press.

Pinker, S. (1994). *The language instinct*. Harmondsworth: Penguin.

Plomin, R. (1994a). Genetic research and identification of environmental influences. *Journal of Child Psychology and Psychiatry, 35*, 817–834.

Plomin, R. (1994b). *Genetics and experience: The interplay between nature and nurture*. London: Sage.

Plomin, R. (1995). Genetics and children's experience in the family. *Journal of Child Psychology and Psychiatry, 36*, 69–112.

Plomin, R., & Bergeman, C.S. (1991). The nature of nurture: Genetic influence on "environmental "measures. *Behavioural and Brain Sciences, 10*, 1–16.

Plomin, R., & DeFries, J.C. (1985). *Origins of individual differences in infancy: The Colorado study*. New York: Academic Press.

Plomin, R., Corley, R., DeFries, J.C., & Fulker, D.W. (1990). Individual differences in television viewing in early childhood: Nature as well as nurture. *Psychological Science, 1*, 371–377.

Plomin, R., DeFries, J.C., & Fulker, D.W. (1988). *Nature and nurture during infancy and middle childhood*. Cambridge: Cambridge University Press.

Plomin, R., & McClearn, G.E. (Eds.) (1993). *Nature, nurture and psychology*. Washington, DC: American Psychological Association.

Plomin, R., Owen, M.J., & McGuffin, P. (1994a). The genetic basis of complex human behaviours. *Science, 264*, 1733–1739.

Plomin, R., Reiss, D., Hetherington, E.M., & Howe, G.W. (1994b). Nature and nurture: Genetic contributions to measures of the family environment. *Developmental Psychology, 30*, 32–43.

Pollard, A., with Filer, A. (1995). *The social world of children's learning*. London: Cassell.

Pound, A., Mills, M., Puckering, C., & Cox, A. (1982). Maternal depression and family functioning. In C.M. Parkes & J. Stevenson-Hinde (Eds.), *The place of attachment in human behaviour*. London: Tavistock.

Puckering, C., Pickles, A., Skuse, D., Heptinstall, E., Dowdney, L., & Zur-Szpiro, S. (1995). Mother–child interaction and the cognitive and behavioural development of four-year-old children with poor growth. *Journal of Child Psychology and Psychiatry, 36*, 573–595.

Radford, J. (1990). *Child prodigies and exceptional early achievers*. Lewes: Harvester.

Radke-Yarrow, M. (1991). The individual and the environment in human behavioural development. In P. Bateson (Ed.), *The development and integration of behaviour*. Cambridge: Cambridge University Press.

Reiss, D., Plomin, R., Hetherington, E.M., Howe, G.W., Rovine, M., Tryon, A., & Hagan, M.S. (1994). The separate worlds of teenage siblings: An introduction to the study of the nonshared environment and adolescent development. In E.M. Hetherington, D. Reiss, & R. Plomin (Eds.), *Separate social worlds of siblings: Impact of nonshared environment on development*. Hillsdale, NJ: Lawrence Erlbaum Associates Inc.

Reynolds, A.J. (1994). Effects of a preschool plus follow-on intervention for children at risk. *Developmental Psychology, 306*, 787–804.

Richards, B. (1994). Child-directed speech and influences on language acquisition: Methodology and interpretation. In C. Gallaway & B.J. Richards (Eds.), *Input and interaction in language acquisition*. Cambridge: Cambridge University Press.

Richman, N., Stevenson, J., & Graham, P. (1982). *Pre-school to school: A behavioural study*. London: Academic Press.

Rodgers, B. (1983). The identification and prevalence of specific reading retardation. *British Journal of Educational Psychology, 53*, 369–373.

Rogoff, B. (1990). *Apprenticeship in thinking*. Oxford: Oxford University Press.

Rogoff, B. (1993). *Guided participation in cultural activity by toddlers and caregivers*. Monographs of the Society for Research in Child Development Vol. 58. Chicago, IL: University of Chicago Press.

Rondal, J.A. (1993). Down's syndrome. In D. Bishop & K. Mogford (Eds.), *Language development in exceptional circumstances*. Hove: Lawrence Erlbaum Associates Ltd.

Rose, R. (1995). Genes and human behaviour. *Annual Review of Psychology, 46*, 625–654.

Rowe, D.C. (1994). *The limits of family influence*. New York: Guilford Press.

Rutter, M. (1985). Family and school influences on cognitive development. *Journal of Child Psychology and Psychiatry, 26*, 683–704.

Rutter, M. (1990) Commentary: Some focus and process considerations regarding effects of parental depression on children. *Developmental Psychology, 26*, 60–67.

Rutter, M. (1992). Nature, nurture and psychopathology: A new look at an old topic. In B. Tizard & V. Varma (Eds.), *Vulnerability and resilience in human development*. London: Jessica Kingsley.

Rutter, M., Maughan, B., Mortimore, P., & Ouston, J. (1979). *Fifteen thousand hours: Secondary schools and their effects on children*. London: Open Books.

Rutter, M., Silberg, J., & Simonoff, E. (1994). Whither behavioural genetics? A developmental psychopathological perspective. In E.M. Hetherington, D. Reiss, & R. Plomin (Eds.), *Separate social worlds of siblings: Impact of nonshared environment on development*. Hillsdale, NJ: Lawrence Erlbaum Associates Inc.

Saxe, G. (1988). The mathematics of street vendors. *Child Development, 59*, 1415–1425.

Saxe, G.B., Guberman, S.R., & Gearhart, M. (1987). *Social processes in early number development*. Monographs of the Society for Research in Child Development Vol. 52. Chicago, IL: University of Chicago Press.

Scarborough, H.S., & Dobrich, W. (1994a). On the efficacy of reading to preschoolers. *Developmental Review, 14*, 245–302.

Scarborough, H.S., & Dobrich, W. (1994b). Another look at parent–preschooler bookreading: How naked is the emperor? *Developmental Review, 14*, 340–347.

Scarr, S. (1992). Developmental theories for the 1990s: Development and individual differences. *Child Development, 63*, 1–19.

Scarr, S. (1993). Biological and cultural diversity: The legacy of Darwin for development. *Child Development, 64*, 1333–1353.

Scarr, S., & McCartney, K. (1983). How people make their own environments: A theory of genotype–environment effects. *Child Development, 54*, 424–435.

Scarr, S., & Weinberg, R.A. (1983). The Minnesota Adoption Studies: Genetic differences and malleability. *Child Development, 54*, 260–267.

Schaffer, H.R. (1992). Joint involvement episodes as context for development. In H. McGurk (Ed.), *Childhood social development*. Hove: Lawrence Erlbaum Associates Ltd.

Schiff, M., Duyme, M., Dumaret, A., & Tomkiewicz, S. (1982). How much could we boost scholastic achievement and IQ scores: A direct answer from a French adoption study. *Cognition, 12*, 165–196.

Schiff M., & Lewontin, R. (1986). *Education and class: The irrelevance of IQ genetic studies*. Oxford: Clarendon Press.

Seglow, J., Kellmer-Pringle, M., & Wedge, P. (1972). *Growing up adopted*. Slough: NFER.

Siegler, R.S. (1983). Information-processing approaches to development. In W. Kessen (Ed.), *Handbook of child psychology*, Vol. 1. New York: John Wiley.

Silva, P., Hughes, P., Williams, S., & Faed, J.M. (1987). Blood lead, intelligence, reading attainment and behaviour in eleven-year-old children in New Zealand. *Journal of Child Psychology and Psychiatry, 29*, 43–52.

Skuse, D. (1984). Extreme deprivation in early childhood. 1: Diverse outcomes for three children in an extraordinary family. 2: Theoretical issues and a comparative review. *Journal of Child Psychology and Psychiatry, 25*, 523–542, 543–572.

Skuse, D. (1993). Extreme deprivation in early childhood. In D. Bishop & K. Mogford (Eds.), *Language development in exceptional circumstances*. Hove: Lawrence Erlbaum Associates Ltd.

Slater, A. (1995). Individual differemces in infancy and later IQ. *Journal of Child Psychology and Psychiatry, 36*, 113–150.

Smetana, J.G., & Kelly, M. (1989). Social cognition in maltreated children. In D. Cicchetti & V. Carlson (Eds.), *Child maltreatment: Theory and research on the causes and consequences of child abuse and neglect*. Cambridge: Cambridge University Press.

Snow, C.E. (1995). Issues in the study of input: Finetuning, universality, individual and developmental differences, and necessary causes. In P. Fletcher & B. MacWhinney (Eds.), *The handbook of child language*. Oxford: Blackwell.

Snow, C.E., Barnes, W.S., Chandler, J., Goodman, I.F., & Hemphill, L. (1991). *Unfulfilled expectations: Home and school influences on literacy*. Cambridge, MA: Harvard University Press.

Sokov, J.L., & Snow, C.E. (1994). The changing role of negative evidence in theories of language development. In C. Gallaway & B.J. Richards (Eds.), *Input and interaction in language acquisition*. Cambridge: Cambridge University Press.

Spitz, R.A. (1946). Anaclitic depression. *Psychoanalytic Study of the Child, 2*, 313–342.

Stafford, L., & Bayer, C.L. (1993). *Interaction between parents and children*. Newbury Park, CA: Sage.

Steinberg, L., Elmen, J., & Mounts, N. (1989). Authoritative parenting, psychosocial maturity, and academic success among adolescents. *Child Development, 60*, 1424–1436.

Sternberg, R.J. (1984). *Mechanisms of cognitive development*. New York: Freeman.

Stevenson, D.L., & Baker, D.P. (1987). The family–school relation and the child's school performance. *Child Development, 58*, 1348–1357.

Stevenson, H.W., Lee, S.-Y., & Stigler, J.W. (1986). Mathematics achievement of Chinese, Japanese and American children. *Science, 231*, 693–699.

Sylva, K. (1994). School influences on children's development. *Journal of Child Psychology and Psychiatry, 35*, 135–170.

Teti, D.M., Gelfand, D.S., Messinger, D.M., & Isabella, R. (1995). Maternal depression and the quality of early attachment: An examination of infants, preschoolers and their mothers. *Developmental Psychology, 31*, 364–376.

Tharp, R., & Gallimore, R. (1988). *Rousing minds to life: Teaching, learning and schooling in social context*. Cambridge: Cambridge University Press.

Thompson, L.A. (1993). Genetic contributions to intellectual development in infancy and childhood. In P.A.Vernon (Ed.), *Biological approaches to the study of human intelligence*. Norwood, NJ: Ablex.

Thompson, R.A. (1994). Emotion regulation: A theme in search of definition. In N.A. Fox (Ed.), *The development of emotion regulation*. Monographs of the Society for Research in Child Development Vol. 59. Chicago, IL: University of Chicago Press.

Tizard, B. (1977). *Adoption: A second chance*. London: Open Books

Tizard, B., Blatchford, P., Farquhar, C., & Plewis, I. (1988). *Young children at school in the inner city*. Hove: Lawrence Erlbaum Associates Ltd.

Tizard, J., Hewison, J., & Schofield, W.N. (1982). Collaboration between teachers and parents in assisting children's reading. *British Journal of Educational Psychology, 52*, 1–15.

Tomasello, M., Conti-Ramsden, G., & Ewert, B. (1990). Children's conversations with their mothers and fathers: Differences in breakdown and repair. *Journal of Child Language, 17*, 115–130.

Tudge, J. (1990). Vygotsky, the zone of proximal development and peer collaboration: Implications for classroom practice. In L.C. Moll (Ed.), *Vygotsky and education.* Cambridge: Cambridge University Press.

Van der Veer, R., & Valsiner, J. (1991). *Understanding Vygotsky: A quest for synthesis.* Oxford: Blackwell.

Vernon, P.A. (Ed.) (1993). *Biological approaches to the study of human intelligence.* Norwood, NJ: Ablex.

Vygotsky, L.S. (1960). The development of higher mental functions. Quoted in J.V. Wertsch (1985). *Vygotsky and the social formation of mind.* Cambridge, MA: Harvard University Press.

Vygotsky, L.S. (1978). *Mind in society: The development of higher psychological processes.* (New edition, edited by M. Cole, V. John-Steiner, S. Scribner, & E. Souberman.) Cambridge, MA: Harvard University Press.

Vygotsky, L.S. (1981). The genesis of higher mental functions. In J.V. Wertsch (Ed.), *The concept of activity in Soviet psychology.* Armonk, NY: M.E. Sharpe.

Vygotsky, L.S. (1986). *Thought and language.* (New edition, edited by A. Kozulin.) Cambridge, MA: Harvard University Press.

Wahler, R.G., & Dumas, J.E. (1989). Attentional problems in dysfunctional mother–child interactions: An interbehavioural model. *Psychological Bulletin, 105*, 116–130.

Weinstein, C.S. (1991). The classroom as a social context for learning. *Annual Review of Psychology, 42*, 493–525.

Wells, C.G. (1985). *Language at home and at school.* New York: Cambridge University Press.

Wertsch, J.V. (1979). From social interaction to higher psychological processes: A clarification and application of Vygotsky's theory. *Human Development, 22*, 1–22.

Wertsch, J.V. (1990). The voice of rationality in a socio-cultural approach to mind. In L.C. Moll (Ed.), *Vygotsky and education.* Cambridge: Cambridge University Press.

Wertsch, J.V. (1991). *Voices of the mind.* London: Harvester.

Wertsch, J.V., McNamee, G.D., McLane, J.B., & Budwid, N.A. (1980). The adult–child dyad as a problem-solving system. *Child Development, 51*, 1215–1221.

Wood, D.J., & Middleton, D.J. (1975). A study of assisted problem-solving. *British Journal of Psychology, 66*, 181–191.

Wood, D.J., Wood, H.A., Griffiths, A.J., Howarth, S.P., & Howarth, C.I. (1982). The structure of conversation with 6–10-year-old deaf children. *Journal of Child Psychology and Psychiatry, 23*, 295–308.

Wood, D.J., Wood, H.A., & Middleton, D.J. (1978). An experimental evaluation of four face-to-face teaching strategies. *International Journal of Behavioural Development, 1*, 131–147.

Woodhead, M. (1985). Pre-school education has long-term effects: But can they be generalised? *Oxford Review of Education, 11*, 133–155.

Woodhead, M. (1988). When psychology informs public policy: The case of early childhood intervention. *American Psychologist, 43*, 443–454.

Yule, W., & Rutter, M. (1985). Reading and other learning difficulties. In M. Rutter & L. Hersov (Eds.), *Child and adolescent psychiatry: Modern approaches.* Oxford: Blackwell.

Zahn-Waxler, C. (1995). Parental depression and distress: Implications for development in infancy, childhood, and adolescence. *Developmental Psychology, 31*, 347–348.

Zahn-Waxler, C., & Kochanska, G. (1990). The origins of guilt. In R.A. Thompson (Ed.), *Socioemotional development*. Nebraska Symposium on Motivation Vol. 36. Lincoln, NE: University of Nebraska Press.

Zigler, E., & Muenchow, S. (1992). *Head Start: The inside story of America's most successful educational experiment*. New York: Basic Books.

Zigler, E., & Styfco, S. (Eds.) (1993). *Head Start and beyond: A national plan for extended childhood intervention*. New Haven, CT: Yale University Press.

Zigler, E., & Valentine, J. (Eds.) (1979). *Project Head Start: A legacy of the war on poverty*. New York: Free Press.

Additional reading

Akhtar, N., Dunham, F., & Dunham, P.J. (1991). Directive interactions and early vocabulary development: The role of joint attentional focus. *Journal of Child Language, 18*, 41–49.

Ceci, S. (1993). Contextual trends in intellectual development. *Developmental Review, 13*, 403–435.

Cherny, S.S. (1994). Home environmental influences on general cognitive ability. In J.C. DeFries, R. Plomin, & D.W. Fulker (Eds.), *Nature and nurture during middle childhood*. Cambridge, MA: Blackwell.

Coon, H., Fulker, D.W., DeFries, J.C., & Plomin, R. (1990). Home environment and cognitive ability of 7-year-old children in the Colorado Adoption Project: Genetic and environmental etiologies. *Developmental Psychology, 26*, 459–468.

Deal, J.E., Halverson, C.F., & Wampler, K.S. (1994). Sibling similarity as an individual differences variable: Within-family measures of shared environment. In E.M. Hetherington, D. Reiss, & R. Plomin (Eds.), *Separate social worlds of siblings: Impact of nonshared environment on development*. Hillsdale, NJ: Lawrence Erlbaum Associates Inc.

Diaz, R.M., Neal, C.J., & Amaya-Williams, M. (1990). The social origins of self-regulation. In L.C. Moll (Ed.), *Vygotsky and education*. Cambridge: Cambridge University Press.

Dumaret, A., & Stewart, J. (1985). IQ, scholastic performance and behaviour of siblings raised in contrasting environments. *Journal of Child Psychology and Psychiatry, 26*, 553–580.

Dunn, J., & Plomin, R. (1990). *Separate lives: Why siblings are so different*. New York: Basic Books.

Dunn, J., & Shatz, M. (1989). Becoming a conversationalist in spite of (or because of) having an older sibling. *Child Development, 60*, 399–410.

Estrada, P., Arsenio, W.F., Hess, R.D., & Holloway, S. (1987). Affective quality of the mother–child relationship: Longitudinal consequences for the child's school-relevant cognitive functioning. *Developmental Psychology, 23*, 210–215.

Ferguson, D.M., Lynskey, M., & Horwood, L.J. (1995). The adolescent outcomes of adoption: A 16-year longitudinal study. *Journal of Child Psychology and Psychiatry, 36*, 597–616.

Laosa, L.M., & Sigel, I. (1982). *Families as learning environments for children.* New York: Plenum Press.

McDonald, L., & Pien, D. (1982). Mother's conversational behaviour as a function of interactional intent. *Journal of Child Language, 9*, 337–358.

McGillicuddy-DeLisi, A., DeLisi, R., Flaugher, J., & Sigel, I. (1987). Familial influences on planning. In S.L. Friedman, E.K. Scholnick, & R.R. Cocking (Eds.), *Blueprints for thinking: The role of planning in cognitive development.* New York: Cambridge University Press.

Olson, S.L., Bates, J.E., & Kaskie, B. (1992). Caregiver–infant interaction antecedents of children's school-age cognitive ability. *Merrill-Palmer Quarterly, 38*, 309–330

Pellegrini, A.D., Masten, A.S., Garmezy, N., & Ferrarese, M.J. (1987). Correlates of social and academic competence in middle childhood. *Journal of Child Psychology and Psychiatry, 31*, 193–201.

Plomin, R., Chipuer, H.M., & Neiderheiser, J.M. (1994). Behavioural genetic evidence for the importance of non-shared environment. In E.M. Hetherington, D. Reiss, & R. Plomin (Eds.), *Separate social worlds of siblings: Impact of nonshared environment on development.* Hillsdale, NJ: Lawrence Erlbaum Associates Inc.

Reynolds, A.J. (1992). Mediated effects of preschool intervention. *Early Education and Development, 3*, 139–164.

Rogoff, B., & Wertsch, J.V. (1984). *Children's learning in the "Zone of Proximal Development".* San Francisco, CA: Jossey-Bass.

Sigel, I.E., McGillicuddy-DeLisi, A.V., & Goodnow, J.J. (Eds.) (1992). *Parental belief systems: The psychological consequences for children*, 2nd edn. Hillsdale, NJ: Lawrence Erlbaum Associates Inc.

Slade, A. (1987). A longitudinal study of maternal involvement and symbolic play during the toddler period. *Child Development, 58*, 367–375.

Snow, C. (1994). Beginning from baby talk: Twenty years of research on input in interaction. In C. Gallaway & B.J. Richards (Eds.), *Input and interaction in language acquisition.* Cambridge: Cambridge University Press.

Stevenson, H.W., Chen, C., Lee, S.-Y., & Fuligni, A.J. (1991). Schooling, culture and cognitive devlopment. In L. Okagaki & R.J. Sternberg (Eds.), *Directors of development: Influences on the development of children's thinking.* Hillsdale, NJ: Lawrence Erlbaum Associates Inc.

Tizard, B., & Hughes, M. (1984). *Young children learning.* London: Open Books.

Wood, D.J. (1989). Social interaction as tutoring. In M.H. Bornstein & J.S. Bruner (Eds.), *Interaction in human development.* Hillsdale, NJ: Lawrence Erlbaum Associates Inc.

Author index

Subject index

For UK/Europe, please send orders to: Erlbaum (UK) Taylor & Francis, Mail Order Department, 27 Church Road, Hove, East Sussex, BN3 2FA, England. Note, prices shown here are correct at time of going to press, but may change. Prices outside Europe may differ from those shown. Please send USA & Canadian orders to: Lawrence Erlbaum Associates Inc., 10 Industrial Avenue, Mahwah, NJ 07430, USA

DEVELOPMENT ACCORDING TO PARENTS

The Nature, Sources and Consequences of Parents' Ideas

JACQUELINE J. GOODNOW (Macquarie University), W. ANDREW COLLINS (University of Minnesota)

"*This is a superb text... Remembering that it is part of a series of essays on child development, I am of the opinion that the organisation of the chapters (the 'story line') couldn't be better. The authors' style is readable and content is erudite without being offputting. I am really impressed by this book and believe it will make a contribution not only to developmental psychology, but also social psychology and my own field, clinical child psychology... The authors, Goodnow and Collins, are to be congratulated.*"
Professor Martin Herbert (Director of Clinical Courses, University of Leicester).

"*Goodnow and Collins have presented us with a timely and unique set of essays on the development and function of parents' ideas. They review a selective body of literature, reflect on knowledge gaps about parents' ideas about the parenting function, and present a detailed research agenda...The chapters flow coherently with discussions of parents ideas and those ideas' characterisations, sources and consequences for parents and children...Goodnow and Collins have performed an exemplary service to the field expressed in their interdisciplinary organization of the study of parents ideas...This book is a must for anyone in the field, irrespective of his or her point of view.*" **Contemporary Psychology;** Reviewed by Irving E. Sigel

To their everyday life with children, parents bring a number of ideas about development and about parenting. Some of these ideas are about their own children and about themselves as parents. Others are more general: ideas, for instance, about what babies are like, how children change with age, what kinds of affection and control they need, the responsibilities of mothers and fathers, or the degree of influence each parent has over the way a child develops. Moreover, the ideas that parents hold, shape their actions with children and the way they assess both their children and their own performance as parents. With the recognition of parental thinking as a powerful factor in family life, research has turned to the study of this 'everyday' or 'informal' psychology. Some of the studies deal with the nature of parents' ideas: What ideas are held? Which are most widely shared? How do these ideas differ from one another? Some deal with the sources of parents' ideas: with the factors that give rise to differences among parents from different backgrounds (different cultures, different economic groups, different degrees of experience with children). Others concentrate on the consequences of parents' ideas for themselves and for children.
0-86377-160-2 1990 150pp. $31.95 £19.95 hbk / 0-86377-161-0 1990 $15.95 £8.95 pbk

*For UK/Europe, please send orders to: Erlbaum (UK) Taylor & Francis, Mail Order Department, 27 Church Road, Hove, East Sussex, BN3 2FA, England. Note, prices shown here are correct at time of going to press, but may change. Prices outside Europe may differ from those shown. **Please send USA & Canadian orders to:** Lawrence Erlbaum Associates Inc., 10 Industrial Avenue, Mahwah, NJ 07430, USA*

APPROACHES TO THE DEVELOPMENT OF MORAL REASONING

PETER E. LANGFORD
(La Trobe University, Victoria, Australia)

The first part of the book offers a survey of current approaches to the development of moral reasoning: those of Freud, ego psychology, Piaget and Kohlberg. The approach of Kohlberg has been popular because he was able to give an impressive account of findings from the key method of interviews, the other crucial method being naturalistic observation of moral discourse. The accounts of interview evidence given by ego psychology and Piaget were less comprehensive and less impressive. Naturalistic studies have either been impressionistic or less detailed in their methods of analysis.

The second part of the book argues that the impressive nature of Kohlberg's later evidence for his view that moral reasoning passes through a sequence of stages is in part illusory, because his theory predicts that specific types of reply will show specific developmental patterns. However, as data are always reported in terms of stages, which amalgamate very disparate types of reply, it is impossible to know whether the specific types of reply follow their predicted developmental courses or not. Reasons given for assigning given types of reply to a stage are also often doubtful. This leads to discussion of studies that have reported findings in terms of specific types of reply (weakly interpretive methods), as opposed to Kohlberg's stage-based and strongly interpretive methods. Findings from these disconfirm Kohlberg's theory at several crucial points.

The second and third parts of the book also examine findings from non-Kohlbergian interviews and other methods, again advocating that weakly interpretive and largely descriptive presentation of findings is preferable to strongly interpretive techniques. It is argued that a wide variety of mechanisms suggested by the theories outlined in the first part of the book, as well as others drawn from general theories of personality development, are able to explain existing descriptive developmental findings. The task for the future is to assess the relative importance of these mechanisms.

Contents: Introduction. Part I: *Theoretical Traditions.* Freud and Erikson. Ego Psychology. Piaget. Kohlberg. Part II: *Interview Findings in the Light of Weakly Interpretive Models.* The Problem Outlined. The Kohlbergian Interview and Weakly Interpretive Scoring. The Other Interview Techniques in the Light of Weakly Interpretive Methods. Part III: *Other Methods.* Findings From Other Methods. Part IV: *Conclusions.* Conclusions and Future Research.

0-86377-368-0 1995 240pp. $39.95 £24.95 hbk

*For UK/Europe, please send orders to: Erlbaum (UK) Taylor & Francis, Mail Order Department, 27 Church Road, Hove, East Sussex, BN3 2FA, England. Note, prices shown here are correct at time of going to press, but may change. Prices outside Europe may differ from those shown. **Please send USA & Canadian orders to:** Lawrence Erlbaum Associates Inc., 10 Industrial Avenue, Mahwah, NJ 07430, USA*